Data Scientist's Book of Quotes

Insights and Advice from Data Science Leaders and Key Influencers

Matt Corey

"When you honour, acknowledge and fully accept your present reality, where you are, who you are, what you are doing right now. When you fully accept what you have got, you are grateful for what you've got, grateful for what is, grateful for being. Gratitude for the present moment at the fullness of life now is through prosperity. It cannot come in the future."

"Acknowledging the good that you already have in your life is the foundation for all abundance."

Eckhart Tolle
Author, The Power of Now and
A New Earth: Awakening to Your Life's
Purpose

"I measure success by how many people love me. And the best way to be loved is to be loveable."

Warren Buffett
Berkshire Hathaway, CEO and Founder

"Warren Buffett has always said the measure [of success] is whether the people close to you are happy and love you…It is also nice to feel like you made a difference-inventing something or raising kids or helping people in need."

Bill Gates, Microsoft Co-Founder

Dedication

To H., whose beautiful soul light, I adore and cherish and to my parents who raised me with the right values and a healthy passion for work.

"I have not failed 1,000 times.
I have successfully discovered 1,000
ways to NOT make a light bulb."

Thomas Edison
Inventor (Phonograph, Motion Picture Camera
and the Electrical Light Bulb) and Businessman

Acknowledgements

I would like to thank all the contributors and their informative, insightful and inspiring contributions within this book.

When I was a younger man, I thought being a successful 'self-made' man was possible. However, I realised with the years passed and life's experiences that one can only become successful with a solid belief system and a clear image of who one is and wishes to become. I can now add, having a sincere and real appreciation of life's offerings (through people and circumstances) and to work with a desire and perseverance to achieve one's goals in life and possess a bigger purpose in life: helping others to become who they wish to become. Accordingly, I agree with Tony Robbins's belief that life is about giving and that providing value is paramount.

Today, with a greater understanding of what is truly important in life, and blessed through my own experiences and challenges, I realise and believe – with a more humble and authentic awareness, that in addition to the above mindset and conditions - to be truly successful and fulfilled in life, is only possible, with life's lessons learned accompanied with the help, guidance, love, support and advice from others: one's friends, loved ones, mentors and simply people who care about you and believe enough in who you are and your dreams.

No person is an island and I can say that I am here at this point in my life, thanks to the help and guidance of others. We all become our real, true self or potential of whom we are meant to become through our interactions and the 'resulting dance of those interactions'. This is one of life's greatest lessons and gift.

I would like to thank all these people, who have helped me learn the above principles through life's experiences and have been there for me and my family. They all know who they are and I respect their privacy. I also thank them for their kind words and gestures at the appropriate times, those moments when they were there for us. I will always remember their acts of kindness and I will appreciate them, until my last day.

A very big thank you and may love and fulfilment always rule supreme in their lives.

Contents

"Life is a gift, and it offers us the privilege, opportunity, and responsibility to give something back by becoming more."

"I've come to believe that all my past failure and frustration were actually laying the foundation for the understandings that have created the new level of living I now enjoy."

Tony Robbins
Author, Entrepreneur, Peak Performance
Coach and Philanthropist

Introduction

I wrote this book, because as a Data Science recruitment professional, I wanted to better understand Data Scientists, Data Science and its related topics from the experts and thought leaders within this field. The original concept grew to become something greater.

Throughout my dealings with Data Scientists, Heads of Data and other Data professionals in the UK, US and Asia, I noticed that we would eventually be discussing the same theme: the human side of being in Data Science and what – beyond the technical aspect – it means to be a Data Scientist. It felt right for me, that with my own experience and background in Human Resources, Recruitment, Psychology and Coaching, that my role is to humanise the way Data Scientist recruitment is done.

What does that actually mean? Being in recruitment, is an enormous responsibility, duty and privilege, because it is one of the most important roles that can ultimately change a person's life and have a corresponding influence on their family, loved ones and their colleagues.

As a result, I am compelled to get it right for my candidate and client, by empowering and guiding both parties in the most professional and caring manner.

It is about this all-important triad consultative-advisory relationship between the candidate, the recruiter and the client. It has to be a best fit for the candidate (based on having the required skills, experience and goal aspirations in their life and work), the client (with their specific requirements of who they need to undertake a certain type of work to meet and exceed the company's expectations and fulfil their customers' needs and wants) and the recruiter (as the intermediary).

Specifically, in a recent study conducted by McKinsey & Co., they surveyed over 1,000 companies across 12 countries and found that a business is likely to perform far better financially, once it has a diverse workforce. As a result, advocating diversity and inclusion (free of bias) could bring enormous benefits and advantages to a business, with happier employees committed to the values and ethos of the organisation.

Surprising to many, the marketplace does actually highly value the non-technical skills and qualities of a Data Scientist, far more than a Data Scientist, who is only great with Statistics or a whiz with Hadoop, Python, R and SQL. The rationale is that they can be trained on the technical skills, in contrast to possessing more effective communication skills, such as showing empathy, listening, being engaging, understanding, an influencer, persuader, a storyteller, being a problem solver and putting forward a business case with the steps forward to reach a successful outcome -based on the data.

This book of over 300 quotes has been my attempt to focus on the personal attributes, skills and qualities of being a Data Scientist and to provide an overview of Data Science and its related fields. The book also contains questions to reflect on at the end of each chapter, relevant resources and recommendations and the potential, risks, opportunities and future of Data Science, along with the many contentious, controversial and legitimate concerns surrounding the field of Data Science.

Data is definitely the new change…the change that is transforming our entire society. Our world will become unrecognisable in the coming years during this Fourth Industrial Revolution. Will it all be good or not? Time will tell in our world of Big Data, Data Governance, the mobile Internet, Cloud computing, the Internet of Things (IoT), Machine Learning, Deep Learning, Artificial Intelligence (AI), Automation, Robotics, Blockchain, Cryptocurrencies, Augmented Reality and much more.

A Data Scientist has one of the key roles that can and will influence senior leadership, stakeholders, staff and customers through the truth of the data. He/she can provide new insights, offer appropriate solutions (based on also having the right questions posed), pinpoint great savings and opportunities through more effective utilisation of resources, examine the obstacles and risks and support the organisation to achieve maximum value, sustainability, impact and customer service excellence.

In addition, a Data Scientist has the added responsibility to help organisations – in this turbulent period of enormous change towards adopting data-driven approaches and behaviours to foster a data-driven culture, in order to reach their digital and business objectives.

As a result, I want to do my part through this book and my efforts, to humanise Data Scientist recruitment by providing candidates who are aware of this responsibility and undertake it with a sense of duty and obligation. For the Data Scientists, to help the organisation by taking on a contributory role of properly communicating and guiding a data-driven culture, promote greater collaboration, share information and insights and explain them for bespoke and varied audiences (including non-technical individuals). Finally, to undertake their work with an authentic, ethical, human-centric and purposeful emotional intelligence, empathy and a broad understanding of the business (and its respective industry) on the pathway to reaching the organisation's growth potential.

35 Reasons to Hire a Data Scientist

1. Ask the right questions to the organisation/business, on what it wants to achieve.

2. Share and communicate insights through the analysis of the data.

3. Introduce, implement and guide data-driven behaviours and actions, leading to a data-driven culture for your organisation/business.

4. Maximise sales and revenue potential and increase overall productivity and profitability.

5. Eliminate waste and duplication of processes leading to savings of labour hours and other resources.

6. Properly collect and analyse the right data for the task at hand.

7. Handle large data sets, when there is too much data for Excel.

8. Can speak directly to clients or other Data Scientists.

9. Take decisions around risk and safeguard your business from risk.

10. Implement procedures and processes to prevent fraudulent transactions.

11. Help with business planning and ensure there is enough adequate data to answer a specific question.

12. Effectively measure your marketing, PR campaigns and social media presence and activities.

13. Recommend what (does and will) drive traffic to your company website.

14. Interpret your customer survey data.

15. Improve the overall customer experience based on the data.

16. Uncover insights from your sales CRM/Database.

17. Analyse the data within the supply chain and sales funnel.

18. Understand your market, competitors and industry (vertical) better.

19. Market to the right customers/clients for your product or service at the right time and through the appropriate mediums.

20. Compare your online presence and market perception profile with your competitors.

21. Measure the efficiency of your HR operations (including the HR systems and software).

22. Analyze your organization's processes, through process optimization metrics.

23. Improve organizational performance (e.g. engagement, staff attrition/turnover, absence, learning and recruitment, in terms of time and cost to hire).

24. Gain greater insight on what is working well on your company website and what to improve.

25. Increase employee performance, efficiency and potential.

26. Analyse the most profitable products and/or services.

27. Data visualization, in order to visualize quantitative data that can then be described with words.

28. Generate timely reports and agreed dashboards to follow on a regular basis (e.g. daily, weekly, monthly, semi-annually and annually).

29. Anticipate unexpected shocks or sudden fluctuations.

30. Gather the data in an appropriate and centralised manner that could become a data mining opportunity.

31. Educate senior management team members on how to express themselves about the data, when talking to new clients.

32. Create a clear distinction between noise and information – random (due to seasonality) or take immediate action.

33. Set up A/B testing – where required, in order to see which option is best and Post A/B testing: for instance, may require adaptability and customization based on the needs of the customer.

34. Conduct a What-if Analysis: estimate when 'x' happens and how it affects 'y'.

35. Perform a Stress Test – this allows you to combine changes and estimate their overall effect quantitatively.

These are only some suggestions on how a Data Scientist can help a small, medium or large business/organisation reach its business potential and how it can also help eradicate diseases, decrease pollution and save people's lives through a greater understanding of the insights uncovered through the exploration of data.

Sources include: Cathy O'Neil's article on 'Why and How to Hire a Data Scientist for your Business' and Beau Walker's Linkedin article on '15 reasons your small business needs a Data Scientist'.

"Your work is going to fill a large part of your life, and the only way to be truly satisfied is to do what you believe is great work. And the only way to do great work is to love what you do.
If you haven't found it yet, keep looking.
Don't settle.
As with all matters of the heart, you'll know when you find it."

Steve Jobs
Designer, Inventor, CEO and Co-Founder,
Apple

"Genius is one percent inspiration and ninety-nine percent perspiration."

Thomas Edison
Inventor (Phonograph, Motion Picture Camera and the Electrical Light Bulb) and Businessman

"You may have to fight a battle more than once to win it."

Margaret Thatcher
Former UK Prime Minister

Chapter 1
What is a Data Scientist?

Definition

"Data Scientist (n.): Person who is better at statistics than any software engineer and better at software engineering than any statistician."

Josh Wills
Director, Data Engineering, Slack

"By 2018, the United States will experience a shortage of 190,000 skilled data scientists, and 1.5 million managers and analysts capable of reaping actionable insights from the big data deluge."

Sebastian Gutierrez
Author, Data Scientists at Work
(Game Changers: Five opportunities for US growth and renewal, McKinsey report)

"Data scientists are kind of like the new Renaissance folks, because data science is inherently multidisciplinary."

John Foreman
Vice President, Product Management, MailChimp

"The "data scientist", which combines the skills of the statistician, software programmer, infographics designer, and storyteller."

Viktor Mayer-Schönberger and Kenneth Cukier
Authors of Big Data: A Revolution That Will Transform How We Live, Work and Think

"A data scientist is someone who can obtain, scrub, explore, model and interpret data, blending hacking, statistics and machine learning. Data scientists not only are adept at working with data, but appreciate data itself as a first-class product."

Hilary Mason
Data Scientist, Accel, Scientist Emeritus,
bitly, Co-Founder, HackNY.
(Originally quoted from Linkedin's Daniel Tunkelang, On
"What is a Data Scientist?", Forbes.

"A data scientist does model-driven analyses of our data; analyzes to improve our planning, increase our productivity, and develop our deeper levels of subject matter expertise. A data scientist works at the tactical, operational, and strategic levels, sharing insights with the business."

Chris Pehura
Practice Director, Management Consultant, C-Suite Data

"As data scientists, our job is to extract signal from noise."

Daniel Tunkelang
Chief Search Evangelist, Twiggle and Consultant

"Good data scientists will not just address business problems; they will pick the right problems that have the most value to the organization.
The data scientist role has been described as "part analyst, part artist.""

Carla Gentry
Data Scientist and Owner, Analytical Solution

"Talented data scientists leverage data that everybody see; visionary data scientists leverage data that nobody see."

Vincent Granville
Author, Executive Data Scientist and Co-Founder,
Data Science Central

"**My** number one piece of advice always is to follow your passions first. Know what you are good at and what you care about, and pursue that...As a successful data scientist, your day can begin and end with you counting your blessings that you are living your dream by solving real-world problems with data."

Kirk Borne
Principal Data Scientist
Booz Allen Hamilton

"**More** generally, a data scientist is someone who knows how to extract meaning from and interpret data, which requires both tools and methods from statistics and machine learning, as well as being human. She spends a lot of time in the process of collecting, cleaning, and munging data, because data is never clean. This process requires persistence, statistics, and software engineering skills — skills that are also necessary for understanding biases in the data, and for debugging logging output from code. Once she gets the data into shape, a crucial part is exploratory data analysis, which combines visualization and data sense. She'll find patterns, build models, and algorithms — some with the intention of understanding product usage and the overall health of the product, and others to serve as prototypes that ultimately get baked back into the product. She may design experiments, and she is a critical part of data-driven decision making. She'll communicate with team members, engineers, and leadership in clear language and with data visualizations so that even if her colleagues are not immersed in the data themselves, they will understand the implications."

Rachel Schutt
Author, Doing Data Science: Straight Talk from the
Frontline

"**D**ata science is an act of interpretation – we translate the customer's "voice" into a language more suitable for decision-making.

A good data scientist is therefore able to get in the mind of people who use our product and understand their needs.

Our distinction between good and great is impact – using insights to influence decisions and ensuring that the decisions had the intended effect."

Riley Newman
General Partner, Wave Capital and Former Head of Data Science, Airbnb

Skills and Qualities

"Service is the rent we pay for being.
It is the very purpose of life and not something you do in your
spare time."

Marian Wright Edelman
Advocate, Children's Rights and Justice for Children

"Free yourself from the bond of convention. Remember, all
human progress is preceded by a new question."

Tony Robbins
Author, Entrepreneur, Peak Performance Coach and
Philanthropist

"**I**'m a data scientist and I'm also an engineer. At the end of the day I want to solve problems. So if I can solve problems today better than I could yesterday, then that's a success."

Kevin Novak
Chief Data Officer, Tala and Former Head of Data Science, Uber

"**W**ithout a grounding in statistics, a Data Scientist is a Data Lab Assistant."

Martyn Jones
Managing Director
Cambriano Energy

"**P**rogramming, Quantitative Analysis, Product Intuition, Communication and Teamwork."

William Chen
Data Scientist, Quora
(Forbes: What Are The Top Five Skills Data Scientists Need?
(Originally on Quora))

"**T**he No. 1 thing is you've got to have passion. This rich passion for going ruthlessly after the problem and being deeply intellectually honest with yourself about whether this is a reasonable answer…

"The second part is having the ability to be extremely clever with the data. And what I mean by that is: You're working with ambiguity.

And very often you can't approach the problem with the rigor you would a homework assignment. The only way to survive through that is by being clever—to think of a different question that gets at the answer."

DJ Patil
Former White House, Deputy Chief Technology Officer for Data Policy and Chief Data Scientist

"[You have to] figure out how to push through and not be frustrated when something doesn't work, because things just don't work most of the time."

Michelangelo D'Agostino
Formerly of President Obama 2012's Data Team

"Key skills are being good listeners, good communicators, sufficient creativity and familiarity with machine learning methods to know how to reframe domain questions as machine learning tasks, the kind of self-scepticism science demands, and the desire to serve as a culture broker between the data and the demands of our collaborators throughout the company."

Chris Wiggins
Chief Data Scientist at the New York Times and Associate Professor of Applied Mathematics at Columbia University

"For me, data science is a mix of three things: quantitative analysis (for the rigor necessary to understand your data), programming (so that you can process your data and act on your insights), and storytelling (to help others understand what the data means)."

Edwin Chen
Founder/CEO
Hybrid AI

"I think how you apply your data science / machine learning skillset matters a great deal. Some people say that "data is just data" and therefore it doesn't matter how they apply their skills, but whether that's a belief you subscribe to or not — everyone is responsible for what they create in this world."

Erin LeDell
Chief Machine Learning Scientist
H2O.ai

"A data scientist as someone "with some mix of coding and statistical skills who work on making data useful in various ways."

"What's special in the Hochster definition is that he categorizes the data scientist in two categories: "Type A" and "Type B.""

Type A for Analysis

Type A Data Scientist: The A is for Analysis. This type is primarily concerned with making sense of data or working with it in a fairly static way. The Type A Data Scientist is very similar to a statistician (and may be one) but knows all the practical details of working with data that aren't taught in the statistics curriculum: data cleaning, methods for dealing with very large data sets, visualization, deep knowledge of a particular domain, writing well about data, and so on.

Type B for Building

Type B Data Scientist: The B is for Building. Type B Data Scientists share some statistical background with Type A, but they are also very strong coders and may be trained software engineers. The Type B Data Scientist is mainly interested in using data "in production." They build models, which interact with users, often serving recommendations (products, people you may know, ads, movies, search results).

Michael Hochster
Head of Research, Pandora
(Originally from a Quora article)

"'Possessed' is probably the right word. I often tell people, 'I don't *want* to necessarily be a data scientist. You just kind of *are* a data scientist. You just can't help but look at that data set and go, 'I feel like I need to look deeper. I feel like that's not the right fit.'"

Jennifer Shin
Director, Data Science, Comcast and Faculty Member, University of California, Berkeley

"Being able to go to subject matter experts and speak the same language goes a long way to gaining credibility and trust from the person with whom you're working."

Eithon Cadag
Senior Data Scientist, Microsoft
(Quoted from The Data Science Handbook)

"Data scientists are involved with gathering data, massaging it into a tractable form, making it tell its story, and presenting that story to others."

Mike Loukides
VP, O'Reilly Media
Author, What is Data Science?

"Being a data scientist is not only about data crunching. It's about understanding the business challenge, creating some valuable actionable insights to the data, and communicating their findings to the business."

Jean-Paul Isson
Global VP Predictive Analytics and BI,
Monster Worldwide Inc.

"You need to be able to take a dataset and discover and communicate what's interesting about it for your users. To turn this into a product requires understanding how to turn one-off analysis into something reliable enough to run day after day, even as the data evolves and grows, and as different users experience different aspects of it."

Amy Heineike
VP Technology, Stealth Startup

"Think analytically, rigorously, and systematically about a business problem and come up with a solution that leverages the available data."

Michael O'Connell
Sr. Director of Analytics, TIBCO
(Quoted from "What Is a Data Scientist?":
Michael O'Connell of TIBCO Spotfire, Forbes)

"Critical thinking skills...really [set] apart the hackers from the true scientists, for me...You must must MUST be able to question every step of your process and every number that you come up with."

Jake Porway
Founder and Executive Director of DataKind

"What sort of personality makes for an effective data scientist? Definitely curiosity…The biggest question in data science is 'Why?' Why is this happening? If you notice that there's a pattern, ask, "Why?" Is there something wrong with the data or is this an actual pattern going on? Can we conclude anything from this pattern?
A natural curiosity will definitely give you a good foundation."

Carla Gentry
Data Scientist and Owner, Analytical Solution

"In the end, the greatest reward…came from what taking a risk demonstrated about me."

Clare Corthell
Creator, The Open Source Data Science Masters

"By definition all scientists are data scientists. In my opinion, they are half hacker, half analyst, they use data to build products and find insights."

Monica Rogati
VP for Data, Jawbone
LinkedIn's Monica Rogati on "What Is a Data Scientist",
Forbes

"As the field grows, keep an open mind and evolve with it. Work hard, think outside the box, and learn as much as you can about the technical side of being a data scientist. Be responsible with the data and realize the potential the data can have to solving problems.
Always ask yourself how the data can be used to positively impact the lives around you, and use that to guide your design and development."

Shanji Xiong
Chief Scientist, Experian's Global DataLab

"As a data scientist, I can predict what is likely to happen, but I cannot explain why it is going to happen. I can predict when someone is likely to attrite, or respond to a promotion, or commit fraud, or pick the pink button over the blue button, but I cannot tell you why that's going to happen. And I believe that the inability to explain why something is going to happen is why I struggle to call 'data science' a science."

Bill Schmarzo
Chief Technology Officer, Dell EMC

"As soon as someone hands you a data set or gives you access to a stream, the very first thing to do is to find an interesting variable in the data set and plot it."

Mike Dewar
Data Scientist, New York Times R&D Lab
(Quoted from The Data Science Handbook)

"The job of the data scientist is to ask the right questions. If I ask a question like 'how many clicks did this link get?', which is something we look at all the time, that's not a data science question.

It's an analytics question. If I ask a question like, 'based on the previous history of links on this publisher's site, can I predict how many people from France will read this in the next three hours?' that's more of a data science question."

Hilary Mason
Founder, Fast Forward Labs

"Statisticians claim that their methods apply to big data. Data scientists claim that their methods do not apply to small data."

Vincent Granville
Author, Executive Data Scientist and Co-Founder, Data Science Central

"What makes a good scientist great is creativity with data, skepticism and good communication skills. Getting all of that together in the same person is difficult—because traditionally, different people follow different paths in their careers—some are more technical, others are more creative and communicative. A data scientist has to have both."

Monica Rogati
VP for Data, Jawbone

"The primary colors of data: hacking skills, math and stats knowledge, and substantive expertise."

Drew Conway
Author, Founder and CEO, Alluvium
and known for his Venn Diagram (of the Data Scientist
having an interaction of the above 3 skills)

"Some of the best data scientists I see often have worked in a few different domains.
I think that helps with creativity and problem solving. A nice way to sum data scientists up that I've heard: 'They're better statisticians than your average programmer and they're better programmers than your average statistician'…on the soft skills side, I'd say they're often very creative, which probably comes from having domain expertise in a number of areas and how they've seen similar problems before. They're able to think of ways to use data to solve problems that otherwise would have been unsolved or solved using only intuition."

Pete Skomoroch
Former Principal Data Scientist, LinkedIn

"Engineering, I think you can pick up.
[A data scientist's] curiosity is built-in."

Scott Nicholson
Former Chief Data Scientist, Accretive Health and Poynt

"Numbers have an important story to tell.
They rely on you to give them a clear and convincing voice."

Stephen Few
Data Visualization Expert, Perceptual Edge

"I always try to look at the problem from the end. When you start from the beginning and everything is blue sky, there are hundreds of ideas to chase as well as thousands of ideas to try and, since everything is possible, nothing ever gets done."

Jonathan Lenaghan
Head of Data Science, PlaceIQ

"Presentation skills are undervalued, but is actually one of the most important factors contributing to personal success and creating successful projects."

Erin Shellman
Statistician and Data Scientist, Nordstrom Data Lab

"Data flows in data sewers. Data scientists process it to make it drinkable, that is, consumable, operationalized."

Vincent Granville
Author, Executive Data Scientist and Co-Founder,
Data Science Central

"The numbers have no way of speaking for themselves. We speak for them. We imbue them with meaning…Data-driven predictions can succeed—and they can fail. It is when we deny our role in the process that the odds of failure rise. Before we demand more of our data,
we need to demand more of ourselves."

Nate Silver
Author and Founder
FiveThirtyEight

"A data scientist must possess the knack of being able to 'identify business value from mathematical models.' But that vital business value can only materialize if the data scientist also networks with other departments, understands their objectives, is familiar with their data and processes – and can spot the analysis options they provide."

Alexander Linden
VP of Data Science, Gartner

"Great data scientists never assume they know something without in-depth analysis, they think in hypotheses which need to be either rejected or proved, and they ask a lot of questions, even if they are 99.9% sure they know the answer."

Karolis Urbonas
Head of Business Intelligence, Amazon Devices, Amazon

Learning

"Who seeks shall find."

Sophocles
Playwright

"We are what we repeatedly do. Excellence, then, is not an act, but a habit."

Aristotle
Philosopher and Scientist

"Autodidacts – the self-taught, uncredentialed, data-passionate people – will come to play a significant role in many organizations' data science initiatives."

Neil Raden
CEO and Principal Analyst, Hired Brains Research

"I joined an open source project, and that was the single best decision in all of graduate school. I learned how to code in a collaborative way."

Chris Moody
Manager of Data Science, Stitch Fix
(Quoted from The Data Science Handbook)

"When it comes to DS (Data Science) education, nowadays there is a lot of emphasis given in one of two things: the math aspect of it, and the complex algorithms of deep learning systems. Although all this is essential, particularly if you want to be a future-proof data science professional, there is much more to the field than that. Namely, the engineer mentality is something that you need to cultivate, since at its core, data science is an engineering discipline. I don't mean that in a software manner, but more of a practicality and efficiency oriented approach to building a system."

Zacharias Voulgaris
Author, Data Scientist
('Why the Engineer Mentality is a Key Part of Data Science')

"**O**nce you have a certain amount of math/stats and hacking skills, it is much better to acquire a grounding in one or more subjects than in adding yet another programming language to your hacking skills, or yet another machine learning algorithm to your math/stats portfolio…Clients will rather work with some data scientist A who understands their specific field than with another data scientist B who first needs to learn the basics—even if B is better in math/stats/hacking."

Stephan Kolassa
Data Science Expert at SAP Switzerland AG

"**Y**ou can best learn data mining and data science by doing, so start analyzing data as soon as you can! However, don't forget to learn the theory, since you need a good statistical and machine learning foundation to understand what you are doing and to find real nuggets of value in the noise of big data."

Gregory Piatetsky-Shapiro
President, KDnuggets

"Many people who come into data science are overwhelmed. They look at the list of "requirements" and think that because they're not a wizard at engineering, or a statistician and a visualizer, that they're not qualified. I think they shouldn't underestimate themselves. I think you should approach things in the T-Shaped model, where you accumulate a great deal of breadth and a concentration in one skill that gives you depth. So be confident and pick up skills; you'll be surprised at how much value you can add immediately."

Diane Wu
Co-Founder and CEO, Genomics
(Quoted from the Data Science Handbook)

"Learning how to do data science is like learning to ski.
You have to do it."

Claudia Perlich
Chief Scientist at Dstillery (formerly Media6Degrees) and teaches Data Mining for Business Intelligence in the MBA program of the Stern School of Business,
New York University

"Data science's learning curve is formidable. To a great degree, you will need a degree, or something substantially like it, to prove you're committed to this career…

Classroom instruction is important, but a curriculum that is 100 percent devoted to reading books, taking tests and sitting through lectures is insufficient.
Hands-on laboratory work is paramount for a truly well-rounded data scientist…

It should not degenerate into a program that produces analytics geeks with heads stuffed with theory but whose diplomas are only fit for hanging on the wall."

James Kobielus
Lead Analyst for Data Science, Deep Learning
and Application Development,
SiliconANGLE Media, Inc.

"Take control of your learning by tailoring it to what you want to do, not the other way around."

Vik Paruchuri
Founder, Dataquest.io

"I do not know how you teach someone to love to learn, but being self-motivated is integral to this field. Once you have the core concepts, to be able to be really excited about, and continue to seek out, new information is something that I look for, for example, when we are recruiting people."

Shelly D. Farnham
Executive Director and Research Scientist,
Third Place Technologies

Questions to Reflect On

Data Scientist: Why am I or want to be a Data Scientist?

Data Scientist: What is my greatest strength or skill as a Data Scientist?

Data Scientist: What areas can I improve on, to reach and exceed expectations, in my current (or upcoming) Data Scientist role?

Hiring Manager: Why do I require a Data Scientist for my organisation/business?

Hiring Manager: What are the essential criteria that I require for this Data Scientist role?

Hiring Manager: How important is it for the incoming Data Scientist to have industry experience (and reasons to support)?

NOTES

"We delight in the beauty of the butterfly but rarely admit the changes it has gone through to achieve that beauty."

Maya Angelou
Poet and Writer

"We must be the change, we wish to see in the world."

Mahatma Gandhi
Activist and Writer

Chapter 2
Power and Potential of Data and Data Science

"Data science is a very rapidly growing field of increasing importance.
So much research and business decisions are based on data. If we want to ask all of the right questions and analyse all aspects of a problem, we need diversity and multidisciplinary thinking."

Margot Gerritsen
Associate Professor of Energy Resources Engineering at Stanford and Director of the Institute for Computational and Mathematical Engineering

"Data Science is huge fun. Poking around a new dataset is the nerd equivalent of exploring the Amazon. Putting your footprint where nobody has stepped before. Discovering a ridiculously colorful new species. Finding interesting and useful things in data is a delicious adventure. And we are blessed to live in a time of easy access to fascinating data, powerful tools, and learning at our fingertips. And all for free. Incredible."

George Roumeliotis
Data Science Manager, Airbnb
(Quoted from his Linkedin article, 'Big Tent Article)

"We're not going to run out of data anytime soon. It's maybe the only resource that grows exponentially. Maybe every 1.5 years we're seeing data double, and much of that data is social data, data about ourselves."

Andreas Weigend
Author, Data for the People: How to Make Our Post-Privacy Economy Work for You and Director, Social Data Lab

"We built a program that can read, find insights and generate human readable output. And we do that at a speed well beyond what just humans can do."

"Once we build machines that help us pass our antiquated cognitive limitations, we're going to free ourselves up to see more of the structure that exists in the world."

Sean Gourley
Founder and CEO, Primer
(Quoted from a Fortune article, "AI Startup Raises Millions to Digest Intel for Spies, Financiers and Walmart")

"Data are becoming the new raw material of business."

Craig Mundie
Former Chief Research and Strategy Officer, Microsoft

"**I** think of data science as more like a practice than a job. Think of the scientific method, where you have to have a problem statement, generate a hypothesis, collect data, analyze data and then communicate the results and take action…
If you just use the scientific method as a way to approach data-intensive projects, I think you're more apt to be successful with your outcome."

Bob Hayes
President, Business Over Broadway and Advisor

"**I** think of data science teams as performing principally either Data Product or Data Impact functions. We've done both, in that we're building a number of data products (so far just for internal use at the NYT) as well as trying to impact roadmaps of other groups. Impact comes from learning models, which are not only predictive but also interpretable.

For example, if we build a model which predicts individual subscribers' likelihood of cancelling, we're interested not only in the machine learning part (does the model predict accurately the at risk individuals), which is an engineering win, but also in the data science win of revealing risky behaviors.

Identifying these suggests changes to product or marketing, which then can be executed and tested."

Chris Wiggins
Chief Data Scientist at the New York Times and Associate Professor of Applied Mathematics at Columbia University

"**D**ata is the sword of the 21st century,
those who wield it the samurai."

Jonathan Rosenberg
Former Senior Vice President for Product Management,
Google

"**D**ata beats emotions."

Sean Rad
Founder of Ad.ly and Tinder

"**U**ber, the world's largest taxi company, owns no vehicles.
Facebook, the world's most popular media owner, creates no
content. Alibaba, the most valuable retailer, has no inventory.
And Airbnb, the world's largest accommodation provider, owns
no real estate. Something interesting is happening. Indeed."

Kevin Kelly
Author of The Inevitable: Understanding the 12
Technological Forces That Will Shape Our Future

"**T**o move towards a data-driven culture, you need a set of social
mechanics that will change the behaviour of people and teams
tangibly every day."

Graham Hogg
Author, Seeing Around Corners and CEO, Connectworxs

"Big data is when the data grows to the point that the technology supporting the data has to change. It also encompasses a variety of topics relating to how disparate data can be combined, processed into insights, and/or reworked into smart products."

Anna Smith
Analytics Engineer, Rent the Runway

"Data science is one of the most exciting and disruptive fields that will radically transform our way of working and living through automation, robotics and the exponential speed of processing data leading to greater awareness and insights."

Matt Corey
Author and Director, Change Force

"In God we trust, all others bring data."

W. Edwards Deming
Professor, Statistician, Author and Consultant

"We were hired to understand how a Trump voter is different from a generic Republican voter. Most modelling is done on a typical Republican versus a typical Democrat, but we knew going into the race that Trump was anything but a typical Republican nominee. He brings a very unique style [and] stance on issues, a different bravado and name ID, so we built all our modelling on who we should talk to and how we should talk to them specifically for his campaign."

"I've worked in [the political] industry for a while now and I've seen a lot of people acting off their gut intuition. There's this thought that just because you've been in an industry for a long time, you have a fundamental understanding of how that industry works, and then data becomes less important because you know all these things."

"But in reality, especially in this election, having a proper understanding of data and what's actually going on allows you to then multiply the power of that intuition and discipline knowledge.

The thing is, Hillary Clinton did actually have really good data scientists working for her campaign too – the big data approach was first seen in Obama's 2012 presidential campaign and used to devastating effect.

So what went wrong?"

"Politics is a blend of art – the art of politics – and data, which is true science. If you put in too much art, you lose the data, and if you put in too much data, you lose the authenticity and message. I think that the combination of art and science is maybe where Hillary got into trouble. I do know she had some fantastic data staff on her team but I'm not sure how much the data spoke for itself and I worry how much political intuition got in the way of true science."

Matthew Oczkowski
Cambridge Analytica's Head of Product, who ran the Trump data campaign (As told to IBTimes UK.)

"The foundation on which a data science team rests is the culture and perception of data elsewhere in the organization. So defining how we think about data has been a prerequisite to ingraining data science in business functions."

Riley Newman
General Partner, Wave Capital and
Former Head of Data Science, Airbnb

"Hiding within those mounds of data is knowledge that could change the life of a patient, or change the world."

Atul Butte
Priscilla Chan and Mark Zuckerberg Distinguished
Professor and Inaugural Director of the Institute of
Computational Health Sciences at the University of
California, San Francisco

"The biggest lesson is to have a very clear set of customers that you're going to serve, notwithstanding the fact you may be building something that can ultimately help many different types of customers."

Roger Ehrenberg
Founder and Managing Partner, IA Ventures

"Unlike statistics, data science uses algorithms rather than models, to make predictions, even to compute confidence intervals."

Vincent Granville
Author, Executive Data Scientist and Co-Founder,
Data Science Central

"You can have data without information, but you cannot have information without data."

Daniel Keys Moran
Programmer and Science Fiction Writer

"The goal is to turn data into information, and information into insight."

Carly Fiorina
Former CEO, HP

"You need statistics to write a research paper, you need data science to optimize a business process."

Vincent Granville
Author, Executive Data Scientist and Co-Founder,
Data Science Central

"Data is the new science. Big Data holds the answers."

Patrick P. Gelsinger
CEO, VMare

"Information is the oil of the 21st century, and analytics is the combustion engine."

Peter Sondergaard
SVP, Gartner Research

"Once we know something, we find it hard to imagine what it was like not to know it."

Chip and Dan Heath
Authors of Made to Stick, Switch

"Data really powers everything that we do."

Jeff Weiner
CEO, Linkedin

"Instincts are experiments. Data is proof."

Alistair Croll and Benjamin Yoskovitz
Authors of Lean Analytics: Use Data to Build a Better Startup Faster

"He who would search for pearls must dive below."

John Dryden
Poet and Playwright

"Data are just summaries of thousands of stories – tell a few of those stories to help make the data meaningful."

Chip and Dan Heath
Authors of Made to Stick, Switch

"More data is better than less.
Otherwise the ideal data set would always be an empty one."

Vincent Granville
Author, Executive Data Scientist and Co-Founder,
Data Science Central

"Not everything that can be counted counts, and not everything that counts can be counted."

Albert Einstein
Physicist and Founder of the Theory of Relativity

"Data isn't information, any more than fifty tons of cement is a skyscraper."

Clifford Stoll
Author, Silicon Snake Oil: Second Thoughts on the
Information Highway

"Most of the world will make decisions by either guessing or using their gut. They will be either lucky or wrong."

Suhail Doshi
CEO, Mixpanel

"It is a capital mistake to theorize before one has data."

Arthur Conan Doyle
Author of Sherlock Holmes stories

"Data science without sustainable, measurable added value,
is not data science.

Data science is the science of producing revenue out of data.
If it does not produce added value, it is not data science."

Vincent Granville
Author, Executive Data Scientist and Co-Founder,
Data Science Central

"...Information, unlike data, is useful. While there's a gulf
between data and information, there's a wide ocean between
information and knowledge. What turns the gears in our brains
isn't information, but ideas, inventions, and inspiration.
Knowledge-not information-implies understanding. And beyond
knowledge lies what we should be seeking: wisdom."

Clifford Stoll
Author, High-Tech Heretic:
Reflections of a Computer Contrarian

"We're entering a new world in which data may be more
important than software."

Tim O'Reilly
Founder, O'Reilly Media

"Data is a precious thing and will last longer than the systems themselves."

Tim Berners-Lee
Inventor of the Worldwide Web

"We've got to use every piece of data and piece of information, and hopefully that will help us be accurate with our player evaluation. For us, that's our life blood."

Billy Beane
General Manager, Oakland As
(Subject of the film, Moneyball)

"Web users ultimately want to get at data quickly and easily. They don't care as much about attractive sites and pretty design."

Tim Berners-Lee
Inventor of the Worldwide Web

"Data is the kind of ubiquitous resource that we can shape to provide new innovations and new insights, and it's all around us, and it can be mined very easily."

David McCandless
Data Journalist

"Data, I think, is one of the most powerful mechanisms for telling stories. I take a huge pile of data and I try to get it to tell stories."

Steven Levitt
Co-Author, Freakonomics

"Before Google, and long before Facebook, Bezos [CEO, Amazon] had realized that the greatest value of an online company lay in the consumer data it collected."

George Packer
Writer, The New Yorker

"Our ability to do great things with data will make a real difference in every aspect of our lives."

Jennifer Pahlka
Founder and Executive Director, Code for America

"It's difficult to imagine the power that you're going to have when so many different sorts of data are available."

Tim Berners-Lee
Inventor of the Worldwide Web

"Some of the best theorizing comes after collecting data because then you become aware of another reality."

Robert J. Shiller
Author, Irrational Exuberance and Winner of the Nobel Prize in Economics

"If you're a scientist, and you have to have an answer, even in the absence of data, you're not going to be a good scientist."

Neil deGrasse Tyson
Astrophysicist

"By relying on the statistical information rather than a gut feeling, you allow the data to lead you to be in the right place at the right time. To remain as emotionally free from the hurly burly of the here and now is one of the only ways to succeed."

James O'Shaughnessy
Chairman and Chief Investment Officer,
O'Shaughnessy Asset Management and Investor

Questions to Reflect On

Maximising the power and potential of Data and Data Science:

Is the organisation/business clear and specific of its goals, targets and vision?

What are we doing with the data in our organisation/business?

Are we fully utilising our Data Scientist(s) to gain maximum insights that could bring increased revenue and profit?

NOTES

"The major value in life is not what you get.
The major value in life is what you become."

Jim Rohn
Author and Motivational Speaker

"Strive not to be a success, but rather to be of value."

Albert Einstein
Physicist and Founder of the Theory of Relativity

Chapter 3
Data and its Value

"You don't need a data scientist to tell you big data is valuable...

You do need one to show you its value."

Dez Blanchfield
Seed Investor and Resident Data Scientist – Market Analyst
(CxO Forum, 2015)

"When your people understand the value of data to the organization, they are much more likely to incorporate it into their decisions in the future. However, you plan to use the data, you want everyone in the organization to be in love with the general idea of using the data."

Bernard Marr
Author of Big Data, Big Data in Practice and Data Strategy

"The world is now awash in data and we can see consumers in a lot clearer ways."

Max Levchin
CEO, Affirm and Former Corporate Director, Yahoo,
Co-Founder and Former CTO of Paypal

"Data, when it's open, it provides transparency."

DJ Patil
Former White House, Deputy Chief Technology Officer
for Data Policy and Chief Data Scientist
(Data Science: Where are we going?,
from the Strata Conference)

"Data Scientists should recall innovation often times is not providing fancy algorithms, but rather value to the customer."

Damian Mingle
Chief Data Scientist, Intermedix

"Data can only be of true value to the organisation and the end user, when it serves the purpose of clarity and understanding of the issues, problems to be resolved and/or the questions asked of it."

Matt Corey
Author and Director, Change Force

"Amazon understands the value of digitizing content, while Google understands the value of datafying it."

"Amazon monitors our shopping preferences and Google our browsing habits, while Twitter knows what's on our minds…and Facebook seems to catch all that information too, along with our social relationships."

Viktor Mayer-Schönberger and Kenneth Cukier
Authors of Big Data: A Revolution That Will Transform
How We Live, Work and Think

"The price of light is less than the cost of darkness."

Arthur C. Nielsen
Market Researcher and Founder of ACNielsen

"In the end, you should only measure and look at the numbers that drive action, meaning that the data tells you what you should do next."

Alex Peiniger
CEO, quintly

"Data science is the key to uncovering insights from data. If used properly, it can help leaders make decisions that may result in an increase of sales, reduction of costs, and provide interesting trends in an organization's data."

Kate Strachnyi
Author, Journey to Data Scientist

"**I** look at a healthy data analytics practice as a three legged stool. All legs have to be equally balanced and strong. The first leg is a team of Data Scientists, mostly with PhDs in disciplines like deep learning. The second leg is Analytics Engineering, folks who help build the production system and scale the production, using tools like Hadoop and Scala.
The third leg is Business Analytics, with folks who can understand the business problems and circle back with Data Scientists and Analytics Engineers."

Pramod Singh
Chief Analytics Officer, Envestnet|Yodlee

"**An** estimate that is slightly biased but robust, easy to compute, and easy to interpret, is better than one that is unbiased, difficult to compute, or not robust. That's one of the differences between data science and statistics."

Vincent Granville
Author, Executive Data Scientist and Co-Founder, Data Science Central

Questions to Reflect On

Is our current data of value to our organisation/business?

How can we get maximum value from our data?

With the insights gathered, how can we best serve and provide real value to our customers?

What questions are we asking to increase our understanding and discover further growth from our data?

NOTES

"You'll see it when you believe it."

Wayne Dyer
Author, "You'll See it When You Believe It"
and Speaker

Chapter 4
Treatment of Data

"The power of treatment of data through an outlier, however random and infrequent a phenomena, still rule. All probabilistic distribution methods and bell-curve and under – or overfitting are meaningless without the grand effects of major outlier events.
Also, developing strong intuitions come when you talk to the janitor, cab driver and avoid echo-chambers of elite scientists."

Tarry Singh
Founder and Researcher deepkapha.ai

"Data that is loved tends to survive."

Kurt Bollacker
Computer Scientist

"Exploratory analysis is what you do to understand the data and figure out what might be noteworthy or interesting to highlight to others."

Cole Nussbaumer Knaflic
Author, Storytelling with Data:
A Data Visualization Guide for Business Professionals

"Tidy datasets are easy to manipulate, model and visualize, and have a specific structure: each variable is a column, each observation is a row, and each type of observational unit is a table. This framework makes it easy to tidy messy datasets, because only a small set of tools is needed to deal with a wide range of un-tidy datasets. This structure also makes it easier to develop tidy tools for data analysis, tools that both input and output tidy datasets."

Hadley Wickham
Chief Scientist, RStudio, Inc

"I believe that, with a few exceptions, less data is more. Once you get beyond some "large enough" number of samples, most models don't really change that much and the additional computation burden is likely to cause practical problems with model fitting."

Max Kuhn
Software Engineer, RStudio, Inc

"Data scientists are involved with gathering data, massaging it into a tractable form, making it tell its story to others."

Mike Loukides
VP, O'Reilly Media

"The bigger goal is to foster a mind-set, so that thinking about data becomes an intellectual first principle, the starting point of inquiry. It's a mentality that can be summed up in a question: What story does the data tell you?"

Steve Lohr
Author, Dataism: The Revolution Transforming Decision Making, Consumer Behaviour, and Almost Everything Else (Inside the Big Data Revolution)

"What does it mean when customers don't take a deal? Does it mean that they didn't want the product as much as they did want the one they bought? Is a negative signal as strong as a positive one? Perhaps they like Champagne but already have a lot in stock. Maybe they just didn't see your e-mail newsletter that month. There are a lot of reasons why someone doesn't take an action, but there are few reasons why someone does. In other words, you should care about purchases, not non-purchases. The fancy way to say this is that there's an "asymmetry" in the data. The 1s are worth more than the 0s. If a customer matches another customer on three 1s, that's more important than matching some other customer on three 0s. What stinks though is that while the 1s are so important, there are very few of them in the data—hence, the term "sparse.""

John W. Foreman
Author, Data Smart: Using Data Science to Transform Information into Insight

"Concentrate on the pearls, the information your audience needs to know."

Cole Nussbaumer Knaflic
Author, Storytelling with Data:
A Data Visualization Guide for Business Professionals

"I don't see the logic of rejecting data just because they seem incredible."

Fred Hoyle
Author and Astronomer

"Predictions based on correlations lie at the heart of big data".

Viktor Mayer-Schönberger and Kenneth Cukier
Authors of Big Data: A Revolution That Will Transform
How We Live, Work and Think

"As data piles up, we have ourselves a genuine gold rush. But data isn't the gold. I repeat, data in its raw form is boring crud. The gold is what's discovered therein."

Eric Siegel
Author, Predictive Analytics: The Power to Predict Who
Will Click, Buy, Lie or Die

"All businesses could use a garden where Data Scientists plant seeds of possibility and water them with collaboration."

Damian Mingle
Chief Data Scientist, Intermedix

"Never again will you simply show data. Rather, you will create visualizations that are thoughtfully designed to impart information and incite action."

Cole Nussbaumer Knaflic
Author, Storytelling with Data:
A Data Visualization Guide for Business Professionals

"Stories don't have graphs.

Real data storytelling is a way to share facts in the form that your listener understands, appreciates and remembers best – the story.

Like any other story, a data story is about a person, a goal, and a challenge. Unlike some other stories, data stories must be true, not just emotionally, but factually. Data stories have the same elements as ordinary stories, backed up by data…
Make your data stories real stories, and align data storytelling with the desires and communication style of your audience."

Meta S. Brown
Author, Data Mining for Dummies
(Originally quoted from Forbes, 'He Turned Data
Storytelling Success Into Data Storytelling Failure.
Here's What Went Wrong.')

"All data has its beauty, but not everyone sees it."

Damian Mingle
Chief Data Scientist, Intermedix

"I think you can have a ridiculously enormous and complex data set, but if you have the right tools and methodology then it's not a problem."

Aaron Koblin
Entrepreneur in Data and Digital Technologies

"In the spirit of science, there is really no such thing as a 'failed experiment.' Any test that yields valid data is a valid test."

Adam Savage
MythBusters Creator

"Theories come and go, but fundamental data always remain the same."

Mary Leakey
Anthropologist

"When human judgment and big data intersect there are some funny things that happen."

Nate Silver
Author and Founder
FiveThirtyEight

Questions to Reflect On

Do you have the right people, tools and methodology to handle the data?

How can technology help us in solving our business challenges?

What story is your data telling you?

Are you data storytelling with the right communication style to your audience?

What are your preferred data visualisation tools?

NOTES

"Learn from the mistakes of others.
You can't live long enough to make
them all yourself."

Eleanor Roosevelt
US Diplomat and Reformer

Chapter 5
Not Having the Right Data

"Data! Data! I can't make bricks without clay!"

Arthur Conan Doyle
Author of Sherlock Holmes stories

"It amazes me how people are often more willing to act based on little or no data than to use data that is a challenge to assemble."

Robert J. Shiller
Author, Irrational Exuberance and Winner of the Nobel Prize in Economics

"Being ignorant of statistics is not compensated by gathering more data."

Vincent Granville
Author, Executive Data Scientist and Co-Founder, Data Science Central

"With too little data, you won't be able to make any conclusions that you trust. With loads of data you will find relationships that aren't real…Big data isn't about bits, it's about talent."

Douglas Merrill
Founder and CEO, ZestFinance

"Without data, you're just another person with an opinion."

W. Edwards Deming
Professor, Statistician, Author and Consultant

"As business leaders we need to understand that lack of data is not the issue. Most businesses have more than enough data to use constructively; we just don't know how to use it.
The reality is that most businesses are already data rich, but insight poor."

Bernard Marr
Author of Big Data, Big Data in Practice and Data Strategy

"I never guess. It is a capital mistake to theorize before one has data. Insensibly one begins to twist facts to suit theories, instead of theories to suit facts."

Arthur Conan Doyle
Author of Sherlock Holmes stories

"Errors using inadequate data are much less than those using no data at all."

Charles Babbage
Mathematician, Inventor, Mechanical Engineer and originally developed the concept of a digital programmable computer

"Without big data analytics, companies are blind and deaf, wandering out onto the Web like deer on a freeway."

Geoffrey Moore
Author of Crossing the Chasm and Inside the Tornado

"A point of view can be a dangerous luxury when substituted for insight and understanding."

Marshall McLuhan
Professor, Author and Philosopher

"Facts do not cease to exist because they are ignored."

Aldous Huxley
Author, Brave New World

"To call in the statistician after the experiment is done may be no more than asking him to perform a post-mortem – he may be able to say what the experiment died of."

Ronald Fisher
Biologist, Geneticist and Statistician

"Data doesn't create meaning, humans do. As my high school algebra teacher used to say, show your math, because if you don't know what steps you took, I don't know what steps you didn't take, and if I don't know what questions you didn't ask. And it means asking ourselves, really, the hardest question of all: Did the data really show us this or does the result make us feel more successful and more comfortable?"

Susan Etlinger
Industry Analyst, Altimeter Group,
Strategic Advisor and Keynote Speaker

"I don't need to know everything about everybody. I just need to know a little bit about a lot of people…If you can get a few bits of information about a lot of people, you can begin to build up a really interesting profile."

Bradley Voytek
UC San Diego Assistant Professor: Cognitive Science,
Neuroscience and Data Science Former Data Scientist, Uber

Questions to Reflect On

Do you require more data or the right data to uncover the insights, leading to action?

Are you rich in data or lacking in insight?

Is your organisation/business working on gut feeling or opinion alone?

Are you applying the right analytics for your data?

How would you handle missing data in a dataset?

NOTES

"Playing it safe is the riskiest choice we can ever make."

Sarah Ban Breathnach
Author, Philanthropist and Public Speaker

Chapter 6
Potential Risks of Data

"Technology is assuming immense importance in this era.
It is said that one who controls data will control the world."

Narendra Modi
Prime Minister of India
(World Economic Forum, January 2018)

"The whole enterprise of teaching managers is steeped in the
ethic of data-driven analytical support. The problem is, the data
is only available about the past. So the way we've taught
managers to make decisions and consultants to analyze problems
condemns them to taking action when it's too late."

Clayton M. Christensen
Management Professor, Harvard University

"One other problem is that too many people-and vendors in
particular-are already using big data to mean any use of
analytics, or in extreme cases even reporting and conventional
business intelligence."

Thomas H. Davenport
Author, Big Data at Work: Dispelling the Myths,
Uncovering the Opportunities

"On average, people should be more skeptical when they see numbers. They should be more willing to play around with the data themselves."

Nate Silver
Author and Founder
FiveThirtyEight

"You can use all the quantitative data you can get, but you still have to distrust it and use your own intelligence and judgement."

Alvin Toffler
Author and Futurist

"The problem with data is that it says a lot, but it also says nothing. 'Big data' is terrific, but it's usually thin. To understand why something is happening, we have to engage in both forensics and guess work."

Sendhil Mullainathan
Professor of Economics, Harvard

"Every second of every day, our senses bring in way too much data than we can possibly process in our brains."

Peter Diamandis
Chairman/CEO
X-Prize Foundation

"Many companies claim they're data-driven. Unfortunately, while they embrace the data part of that mantra, few focus on the second word: driven. If you have a piece of data on which you cannot act, it's a vanity metric."

Alistair Croll
Author, Lean Analytics: Use Data to Build a
Better Startup Faster

"Data adds concrete information to a teacher's observations and intuition, but it will never replace experience, personal relationships, and cultural understanding."

Jose Ferreira
Founder and CEO, Knewton

Questions to Reflect On

Are your insights free of cultural and diversity bias, groupthink and silo thinking?

Are you able to process the data fast enough and take appropriate actions for maximum positive value and impact?

Is your organisation/business, a data culture or a data-driven culture?

There is a potential risk of analysing something, which offers useless results. What could you do, to be free of this?

NOTES

"The ultimate measure of a man is not where he stands in moments of comfort and convenience, but where he stands at times of challenge and controversy."

Martin Luther King, Jr.
Minister and Leader in the Civil Rights
Movement

"We need diversity of thought in the world to face the new challenges."

Tim Berners-Lee
Inventor of the World Wide Web

"In science it often happens that scientists say, 'You know that's a really good argument' my position is mistaken,' and then they would actually change their minds and you never hear that old view from them again. They really do it. It doesn't happen as often as it should, because scientists are human and change is sometimes is painful. But it happens every day. I cannot recall the last time something like that happened in politics or religion."

Carl Sagan
Author, Astronomer, Astrophysicist and Cosmologist

Chapter 7
Challenges within Data

"One of the big challenges of being a data scientist that people might not usually think about – is that the results or the insights you come up with have to make sense and be convincing. The more intelligible you can make them, the more likely it is that your recommendations will be put into effect."

Victor Hu
Head of Data Science, QBE Insurance

"Conversations that happen in machines are different from the ones that happen in the physical world. In the physical world, it lasts a long time and we are able to use a lot of cues other than just text or audio. In computers, interactions are usually very short and many times there are many more people involved."

Andre Karpistsenko
Co-Founder and Research Lead, Planet OS

"There is no bottleneck for data scientists…The bottleneck is very often for companies who don't have a culture of working with data to actually cut down the process into the right steps."

Lutz Finger
Director of Data Science, Snap

"My primary challenge as a data scientist is to use the right algorithm to connect the right data to the problem you actually want solved."

Claudia Perlich
Chief Scientist at Dstillery (formerly Media6Degrees) and teaches Data Mining for Business Intelligence in the MBA program of the Stern School of Business, New York University

"Big data will spell the death of customer segmentation and force the marketer to understand each customer as an individual within 18 months or risk being left in the dust."

Ginni Rometty
CEO, IBM

"A data-driven culture can arise, when the organisation, as a whole, starting from the top to the bottom, understand and accept that from raw data to smart data, an organisation can be empowered to reach new heights and surpass all precedents."

Matt Corey
Author and Director, Change Force

"A significant constraint on realizing value from Big Data will be a shortage of talent, particularly of people with deep expertise in statistics and machine learning, and the managers and analysts who know how to operate companies by using insights from Big Data."

McKinsey Report
Big Data: The next frontier for innovation,
competition and productivity

"Good data science is exactly the same [as] good science...Good data science will never be measured by the terabytes in your Cassandra database, the number of EC2 nodes your jobs is using, or the volume of mappers you can send through a Hadoop instance.
Having a lot of data does not license you to have a lot to say about it."

Drew Conway
Founder and CEO, Alluvium

"Companies struggle with volumes of data and money spent on sourcing, storing, and managing huge volumes of data. Unfortunately, they also struggle to keep up with the value and monetization of data. When it comes to using Big Data, the adage of 'dream big and smart' holds truer than ever."

Uma Talreja
Chief Digital Officer, Raymond

"Men and machines are good at different things. People form plans and make decisions in complicated situations. We are less good at making sense of enormous amounts of data. Computers are exactly the opposite: they excel at efficient data processing but struggle to make basic judgments that would be simple for any human."

Peter Thiel
Author, Zero to One: Notes on Starts Ups,
or How to Build the Future

"The ability to capture end to end customer information is the biggest challenge for a retailer. The ability to merge structured and unstructured data into an Analytics Platform and be able to generate cohorts effectively is a challenge in today's landscape. There is a sudden surge of data and ability to manage the same and generate meaning out of the same is a challenge."

Piyush Kumar Chowhan
VP and CIO
Arvind Lifestyle Brands

"Organizations need to operate at the intersection of data-driven behaviours and their purpose."

Graham Hogg
Author, Seeing Around Corners and CEO, Connectworxs

"We are generating more data than ever before – 90% of the data that we have today is generated in the last 2 years alone. This data is coming from a variety of different sources such as voice, text, transaction, sensor, chat, images, videos, etc. To handle this fast moving, heterogeneous and multimodal data we need to get more entrenched with machine learning and deep learning to make real time analytics driven decisions that will bring maximum value for the customers and companies alike."

Ratnakar Pandey
Analytics and Data Science Head, Kabbage

"When I was a young analyst, people struggled to understand what relevance data had in their lives. Using the word "data" was the quickest way to end a social conversation. I think people outside the analytic world still struggle with the exact relevance of data, however, they have a growing awareness that it is important."

Chris Arnold ('The Data Whisperer')
Knowledge Services Leader
Wells Fargo

"Being into the analytics space for almost a decade now, I have witnessed tremendous transformation from business intelligence to using advanced analytics, for driving business decisions and developing various marketing campaigns. The talent pool is limited which drives the nicheness in the market, and demand is surging as we progress."

Jatin Solanki
Head of Analytics
Coverfox Insurance

"The availability of all this data means that virtually every business or organizational activity can be viewed as a big data problem or initiative. Manufacturing, in which most machines already have one or more microprocessors, is increasingly a big-data environment. Consumer marketing, with myriad customer touchpoints and clickstreams, is already a big data problem. Google has even described its self-driving cars as a big-data project."

Thomas H. Davenport
Author, Keeping Up with the Quants:
Your Guide to Understanding and Using Analytics

"There were 5 exabytes of information created between the dawn of civilization through 2003, but that much information is created every 2 days."

Eric Schmidt
Former Executive Chairman of Google and Alphabet

"How do you merge data with human decision-making? It's one of the harder areas in data science."

Caitlin Smallwood
VP of Science and Algorithms, Netflix

Questions to Reflect On

What are your challenges with the data in your organisation/business?

Are we asking the right questions in solving business problems?

Once you impart information from the data, are you putting forth the appropriate actions?

With a given dataset, how will you go about its suitability to the business problem at hand?

NOTES

"Education is the key to unlocking the world, a passport to freedom."

Oprah Winfrey
Media Owner, Talk Show Host, Author and
Philanthropist

Chapter 8
Machine Learning

"Over the past decades computers have broadly automated tasks that programmers could describe with clear rules and algorithms. Modern machine learning techniques now allow us to do the same for tasks where describing the precise rules is much harder."

"But much of what we do with machine learning happens beneath the surface. Machine learning drives our algorithms for demand forecasting, product search ranking, product and deals recommendations, merchandising placements, fraud detection, translations, and much more. Though less visible, much of the impact of machine learning will be of this type — quietly but meaningfully improving core operations."

Jeff Bezos
CEO, Amazon
(Shareholder Letter in 2017)

"What I see is an AI first world, and for every customer…to be able to get a whole another generation of productivity out of artificial intelligence, machine learning and deep learning."

Marc Benioff
CEO, Salesforce

"The human condition is plagued with a labyrinth of shortcomings, frailties and limitations that hinder man from reaching his fullest potential. Therefore, it only makes sense that we find ourselves at the next phase in human evolution where restricted man merges with the infinite possibilities of hyper-evolving technologies. This techno-human transmutation will prove to be 'the' quantum leap in human progression. The harmonization of technologically extending oneself, consciousness, artificial intelligence and machine learning will reverse the failures of genetic predisposition and limitation."

James Scott
Senior Fellow, Institute for Critical Infrastructure Technology

"Machine intelligence is the last invention that humanity will ever need to make."

Nick Bostrom
Philosopher and Futurist

"Generative Adversial Networks is the most interesting idea in the last ten years in machine learning."

Yann LeCun
Chief AI Scientist, Facebook

"We are starting to see new companies applying machine learning to healthcare in highly innovative and exciting ways. For example, Jeremy Howard's Enlitic is applying deep learning to medical imaging. The more successful examples that we have of this type of thing, the more that will inspire data scientists to leave their ad-click jobs for careers that lead to curing cancer."

Erin LeDell
Chief Machine Learning Scientist
H2O.ai

"(Users) give us a signal and then machines take that input and effectively use machine-learning models to find out what your tastes are and try to get you to have an affinity for it."

Shiva Rajaraman
Product Leader, Investor and Advisor

"All machine learning creates false positives, but the focus of the study was to measure the deep learning models against human performance."

Curt Davis
Director, Center for Geospatial Intelligence (CGI)

"Cyber hygiene, patching vulnerabilities, security by design, threat hunting and machine learning based artificial intelligence are mandatory prerequisites for cyber defense against the next generation threat landscape."

James Scott
Senior Fellow, The Center for Cyber Influence Operations Studies

"In the past, Apple has not been at the vanguard of machine learning and cutting edge artificial intelligence work, but that is rapidly changing, they are after the best and the brightest, just like everybody else."

Oren Etzioni
CEO, Allen Institute for Artificial Intelligence

"In a way, AI is both closer and farther off than we imagine. AI is closer to being able to do more powerful things than most people expect – driving cars, curing diseases, discovering planets, understanding media. Those will each have a great impact on the world, but we're still figuring out what real intelligence is."

Mark Zuckerberg
CEO, Facebook

"We should be able to use the same base system and do air quality forecasting in different parts of the world, with the machine-based learning we can do it very quickly."

Brad Gammons
Green Horizon Global Business Initiative Leader, IBM

"The human condition is plagued with a labyrinth of shortcomings, frailties and limitations that hinder man from reaching his fullest potential. Therefore, it only makes sense that we find ourselves at the next phase in human evolution where restricted man merges with the infinite possibilities of hyper-evolving technologies. This techno-human transmutation will prove to be 'the' quantum leap in human progression. The harmonization of technologically extending oneself, consciousness, artificial intelligence and machine learning will reverse the failures of genetic predisposition and limitation."

James Scott
Senior Fellow, The Center for Cyber Influence Operations Studies

"We are going to completely change what it means to do advanced analytics with our data solutions. We have machine-learning stuff that is about really bringing advanced analytics and statistical machine learning into data-science departments everywhere."

Satya Nadella
CEO, Microsoft

"We think machine learning, as it relates to healthcare and life sciences, is extraordinary."

Ruth Porat
CFO, Alphabet

"Cyber hygiene, patching vulnerabilities, security by design, threat hunting and machine learning based artificial intelligence are mandatory prerequisites for cyber defense against the next generation threat landscape."

James Scott
Senior Fellow, Institute for Critical Infrastructure Technology

"One of the things we did at PayPal was collaborative filtering and machine learning: looking at patterns of human behavior. We used it there to predict when people would try to cheat the system to get money. But you can predict pretty much any behavior with a certain amount of accuracy."

Max Levchin
CEO, Affirm and Former Corporate Director, Yahoo, Co-Founder and Former CTO of Paypal

"There's a new set of transformative technologies such as machine learning, AI, and virtual reality that will spawn another set of big tech franchises. But in terms of cultural impact, perhaps we are at peak Valley."

Brad Stone
Tech Journalist and Author, The Everything Store
and The Upstarts

"Predictive modelling generates the entire model from scratch. All the model's math or weights or rules are created automatically by the computer. The machine learning process is designed to accomplish this task, to mechanically develop new capabilities from data. This automation is the means by which PA [Predictive Analytics] builds its predictive power."

Eric Siegel
Author, Predictive Analytics: The Power to Predict Who
Will Click, Buy, Lie or Die

"Machine learning is the science of getting computers to learn without being explicitly programmed."

Sebastian Thrun
CEO, Kitty Hawk Corporation, Chairman and
Co-Founder, Udacity and Former Google VP

"Computer vision and machine learning have really started to take off, but for most people, the whole idea of what is a computer seeing when it's looking at an image is relatively obscure."

Mike Krieger
Co-Founder, Instagram

"When you apply computer science and machine learning to areas that haven't had any innovation in 50 years, you can make rapid advances that seem really incredible."

Bill Maris
Former Google Ventures Founder, President and CEO

"Signature-based malware detection is dead. Machine learning based Artificial Intelligence is the most potent defense the next gen adversary and the mutating hash."

James Scott
Senior Fellow, Institute for Critical Infrastructure Technology

"The science of machine learning is largely experimental because no universal learning algorithm exists--none can enable the computer to learn every task it is given well. Any knowledge-acquisition algorithm needs to be tested on learning tasks and data specific to the situation at hand, whether it is recognizing a sunset or translating English into Urdu. There is no way to prove that it will be consistently better across the board for any given situation than all other algorithms."

Yoshua Bengio
"Machines Who Learn", Scientific American, June 2016

"In 'Chappie,' you see this sort of young robot that's learning through maybe 'deep learning' how to see the world really, look out into the world, and learn step by step. What's so interesting is that with 'Chappie,' you're getting to see how human behavior reacts to artificial intelligence, and I don't think it's always going to be positive."

Gray Scott
Futurist and Techno-Philosopher

Questions to Reflect On

Can you think of one of your preferred machine learning algorithms and the reasons for your choice?

How would you evaluate the effectiveness of a machine learning model?

What is a popular application of machine learning that you see on a regular basis?

What machine learning skills could someone use to increase sales and profit?

NOTES

"Education is for improving the lives of others and for leaving your community and world better than you found it."

Marian Wright Edelman
Advocate, Children's Rights and Justice for Children

Chapter 9
Deep Learning

"**I** think people need to understand that deep learning is making a lot of things, behind-the-scenes, much better. Deep learning is already working in Google search, and in image search; it allows you to image search a term like "hug.""

Geoffrey Hinton
Cognitive Psychologist and Computer Scientist

"**M**achine learning allows us to build software solutions that exceed human understanding and shows us how AI can innervate every industry."

Steve Jurvetson
Businessman and Venture Capitalist Investor

"**I**n deep learning, the algorithms we use now are versions of the algorithms we were developing in the 1980s, the 1990s. People were very optimistic about them, but it turns out they didn't work too well."

Geoffrey Hinton
Cognitive Psychologist and Computer Scientist

"We wanted to test these deep learning methods on a realistic, real-world analysis problem to critically assess their utility and potential impact, the results were much better than we anticipated. Historically, machine learning algorithms haven't performed well when they have been applied to large satellite imagery datasets."

Curt Davis
Director, Center for Geospatial Intelligence (CGI)

"The deep learning techniques, while relatively easy to learn, are quite foreign to traditional engineering modalities. It takes a different mindset and a relaxation of the presumption of control. The practitioners are like magi, sequestered from the rest of a typical engineering process."

Steve Jurvetson
Businessman and Venture Capitalist Investor

"The analogy to deep learning [one of the key processes in creating artificial intelligence] is that the rocket engine is the deep learning models and the fuel is the huge amounts of data we can feed to these algorithms."

Andrew Ng
Former Chief Scientist, Baidu
Co-Founder and Chairman, Coursera

"With Data Science and Deep Learning community going deeper into their specializations, it is critical to take a step back and understand not only the "machine learning tribes behaviour", but also gain more insights and intuitions to solving problems in the fields of AI."

Tarry Singh
Founder and Researcher, deepkapha.ai

"By developing deep learning solutions that are faster, easier, and less expensive to use, Nervana is democratizing deep learning and fuelling advances in medical diagnostics, image and speech recognition, genomics, agriculture finance, and eventually across all industries."

Steve Jurvetson
Businessman and Venture Capitalist Investor

"Whatever you are studying right now, if you are not getting up to speed on deep learning, neural networks, etc., you lose. We are going through the process, where software will automate software, automation will automate automation."

Mark Cuban
Author, Businessman and Investor

"Most companies are looking at real-time analytics and real-time decision-making. Machine learning and artificial intelligence are the key innovative areas in this space today. Earlier, few companies were using ML and Data Science, but now with the availability of cheap computing power it has become mainstream."

Arun Singhal
Product Manager, Data and Analytics Division, Intuit

Questions to Reflect On

Is deep learning driving your algorithms?

What is the difference between deep learning and machine learning?

How does deep learning relate to your organisation/business?

What are your favourite resources, books or papers on machine learning and deep learning?

NOTES

"If I have seen farther than others, it is because I have stood on the shoulders of giants."

Isaac Newton
Mathematician, Astronomer,
Author and Physicist

"If the rate of change on the outside exceeds the rate of change on the inside, the end is near."

Jack Welch
Author and Former CEO, General Electric

Chapter 10
Artificial Intelligence

"AI will be more important than fire or electricity for humans."

Sundar Pichai
CEO, Google

"Humans should do zero percent of the hard and boring work, computers the rest."

Jürgen Schmidhuber
Director and Professor, IDSIA
Co-Founder and Chief Scientist, NNAISENSE

"A strategy in which you do AI for AI's sake will never work – you have to drive towards a solution from an initial customer pain. That's how all great companies are built!"

Dennis R. Mortensen
Founder, X.ai

"**AI** is probably the most important thing that humanity has ever worked on and I think it is more profound than electricity or fire. It may make it possible for us to have clean, cheap and renewable energy for the future. Take education for example, it's really difficult to educate people in a cost effective way. AI may fundamentally change that equation…The risks are important and the way we solve it is by thinking ahead. We worry about it. We do things like being upfront, have ethical charters. Think about AI safety from day one. Be transparent and open about how we pursue progress there…Countries, we have agree to demilitarise AI and I think that's a common goal, countries should work towards."

Sundar Pichai
CEO, Google

"**Artificial Intelligence is the new electricity.**"

Andrew Ng
Former Chief Scientist, Baidu
Co-Founder and Chairman, Coursera

"**…AI** is not as widespread as many would like. The reality is that there are only a handful of companies — technology giants such as Facebook, Google, and Uber — that have tapped into the promise of AI and actually accomplishing their goals with it. Most companies continue to struggle with adopting AI for several reasons, including that AI problems in many businesses are often *harder* than AI problems on the web, and lack of suitable technology platforms and expertise."

Matei Zahaira
Chief Technologist, Databricks

"As long as there is an AI shortcoming in any such area of endeavor, skeptics will point to that area as an inherent bastion of permanent human superiority over the capabilities of our own creations. This book will argue, however, that within several decades information-based technologies will encompass all human knowledge and proficiency, ultimately including the pattern-recognition powers, problem-solving skills, and emotional and moral intelligence of the human brain itself."

Ray Kurzweil
Author, The Singularity is Near:
When Humans Transcend Biology

"I'm increasingly to think that there should be some regulatory oversight, maybe at the national and international level, just to make sure that we don't do something very foolish. I mean with artificial intelligence we're summoning the demon."

Elon Musk
CEO of Tesla, SpaceX and Co-Founder of Paypal

"Just as electricity transformed almost everything 100 years ago, today I actually have a hard time thinking of an industry that I don't think AI (Artificial Intelligence) will transform in the next several years."

Andrew Ng
Former Chief Scientist, Baidu
Co-Founder and Chairman, Coursera

"If aliens visit us, the outcome would be similar to the arrival of Christopher Columbus in America, an event that did not bring anything good for American natives.

The development of full artificial intelligence could spell the end of the human race...
It would take off on its own, and re-design itself at an ever-increasing rate. Humans, who are limited by slow biological evolution, couldn't compete, and would be superseded."

Stephen Hawking
Professor and Author

"I think AI is akin to building a rocket ship. You need a huge engine and a lot of fuel. If you have a large engine and a tiny amount of fuel, you won't make it to orbit. If you have a tiny engine and a ton of fuel, you can't even lift off. To build a rocket you need a huge engine and a lot of fuel."

Andrew Ng
Former Chief Scientist, Baidu
Co-Founder and Chairman, Coursera

"The pace of progress in artificial intelligence (I'm not referring to narrow AI) is incredibly fast. Unless you have direct exposure to groups like Deepmind, you have no idea how fast-it is growing at a pace close to exponential. The risk of something seriously dangerous happening is in the five-year timeframe. 10 years at most."

Elon Musk
CEO of Tesla, SpaceX and Co-Founder of Paypal

"There is no reason and no way that a human mind can keep up with an artificial intelligence machine by 2035."

Gray Scott
Futurist Philosopher

"Artificial intelligence will reach human levels by around 2029. Follow that out further to, say, 2045, we will have multiplied the intelligence, the human biological machine intelligence of our civilization a billion-fold."

Ray Kurzweil
Author, The Singularity is Near:
When Humans Transcend Biology

"Artificial Intelligence will create smart machines that will destroy a huge swath of jobs currently done by humans."

Gregory Piatetsky-Shapiro
Co-Founder, KDD (Knowledge Discovery and
Data Mining Conferences)

"The real question is, when will we draft an artificial intelligence bill of rights? What will that consist of? And who will get to decide that?"

Gray Scott
Futurist Philosopher

"The upheavals [of artificial intelligence] can escalate quickly and become scarier and even cataclysmic. Imagine how a medical robot, originally programmed to rid cancer, could conclude that the best way to obliterate cancer is to exterminate humans who are genetically prone to the disease."

Nick Bilton
Tech Columnist, New York Times

"I don't want to really scare you, but it was alarming how many people I talked to who are highly placed people in AI who have retreats that are sort of 'bug out' houses, to which they could flee if it all hits the fan."

James Barrat
Author, Our Final Invention: Artificial Intelligence
and the End of the Human Era

"The reason I say that I don't worry about AI turning evil is the same reason I don't worry about overpopulation on Mars. Hundreds of years from now I hope we've colonized Mars. But we've never set foot on the planet so how can we productively worry about this problem now?"

Andrew Ng
Former Chief Scientist, Baidu
Co-Founder and Chairman, Coursera

"Some people call this artificial intelligence, but the reality is this technology will enhance us. So instead of artificial intelligence, I think we'll augment our intelligence."

Ginni Rometty
Chairwoman, President and CEO of IBM

"Google. The ultimate search engine that would understand everything on the web.
It would understand exactly what you wanted, and it would give you the right thing. We're nowhere near doing that now. However, we can get incrementally closer to that, and that is basically what we work on."

Larry Page
Co-Founder, Google

"We must address, individually and collectively, moral and ethical issues raised by cutting edge research in artificial intelligence and biotechnology, which will enable significant life extension, designer babies, and memory extraction."

Klaus Schwab
Engineer, Economist and Founder and Executive Chairman of the World Economic Forum

"Whoever perceives that robots and artificial intelligence are merely here to serve humanity, think again. With virtual domestic assistants and driverless cars just the latest in a growing list of applications, it is we humans who risk becoming dumbed down and ultimately subservient to machines."

Alex Morritt
Author, Impromptu Scribe

"If the government regulates against use of drones or stem cells or artificial intelligence, all that means is that the work and the research leave the borders of that country and go someplace else."

Peter Diamandis
Chairman/CEO
X-Prize Foundation

"We've been redefining what it means to be human. Over the past 60 years, as mechanical processes have replicated behaviors and talents we thought were unique to humans, we've had to change our minds about what sets us apart. As we invent more species of AI, we will be forced to surrender more of what is supposedly unique about humans. Each step of surrender—we are not the only mind that can play chess, fly a plane, make music, or invent a mathematical law—will be painful and sad. We'll spend the next three decades—indeed, perhaps the next century—in a permanent identity crisis, continually asking ourselves what humans are good for. If we aren't unique toolmakers, or artists, or moral ethicists, then what, if anything, makes us special? In the grandest irony of all, the greatest benefit of an everyday, utilitarian AI will not be increased productivity or an economics of abundance or a new way of doing science—although all those will happen. The greatest benefit of the arrival of artificial intelligence is that AIs will help define humanity. We need AIs to tell us who we are."

Kevin Kelly
Author of The Inevitable: Understanding the 12 Technological Forces That Will Shape Our Future

Questions to Reflect On

Is Artificial Intelligence, a part of your data strategy?

If yes, in what areas?

Could AI replace all human knowledge and proficiency and having humans being subservient to machines?

Would it make sense to create a national and international regulatory body or an AI Bill of Rights to oversee the current use of AI?

Is AI a blessing or a threat to jobs currently done by people?

Why would we need AI to define our humanity?

NOTES

"Historically, privacy was almost implicit, because it was hard to find and gather information. But in the digital world, whether it's digital cameras or satellites or just what you click on, we need to have more explicit rules – not just for governments but for private companies."

Bill Gates
Author and Co-Founder of Microsoft

"Civilization is the progress toward a society of privacy. The savage's whole existence is public, ruled by the laws of his tribe. Civilization is the process of setting man free from men."

Ayn Rand
Author

Chapter 11
Data Ethics and Data Privacy

"If today's social media has taught us anything about ourselves as a species, it is that the human impulse to share overwhelms the human impulse for privacy."

Kevin Kelly
Author, The Inevitable: Understanding the 12 Technological Forces That Will Shape Our Future

"How do we start to regulate the mathematical models that run more and more of our lives? I would suggest that the process begin with the modelers themselves.
Like doctors, data scientists should pledge a Hippocratic Oath, one that focuses on the possible misuses and misinterpretations of their models."

Cathy O'Neil
Author, Weapons of Math Destruction:
How Big Data Increases Inequality and
Threatens Democracy

"Everything we do in the digital realm – from surfing the Web to sending an e-mail to conducting a credit card transaction to, yes, making a phone call – creates a data trail.
And if that trail exists, chances are someone is using it – or will be soon enough."

Douglas Rushkoff
Author, Throwing Rocks at the Google Bus

"Some people have been taking data for many years after you gave them permission and have stopped using the product…I don't think clients understand what data's being taken and how it's being used.

Is the data being resold? Was that part of the original deal? If it is resold, then liability issues can arise.

"If you wake up tomorrow and there's no money in your bank account, that's my problem. But if you gave your passcode away to a company and that company itself did something wrong, that's your problem…"

Jamie Dimon
Chairman, President and CEO, JP Morgan Chase
(Fortune Magazine article, May 23, 2016)

"You happily give Facebook terabytes of structured data about yourself, content with the implicit tradeoff that Facebook is going to give you a social service that makes your life better."

John Battelle
Founder, Wired Magazine

"It's so cheap to store all data. It's cheaper to keep it than to delete it. And that means people will change their behaviour because they know anything they say online can be used against them in the future."

Mikko Hypponen
Security and Privacy Expert

"The price of freedom is eternal vigilance. Don't store unnecessary data, keep an eye on what's happening, and don't take unnecessary risks."

Chris Bell
US Congressman

"...With the commitment to create a Centre for Data Ethics and Innovation, the (UK) government is putting ethics at the heart of how this country develops and harnesses the power of AI and automation.

It is important to remember that technology is essentially neutral.

We need more public trust to free our data to generate the growth and welfare. Data sharing is a social benefit. It is the way value is created in the AI era.

In fact, data sharing should be part of the "social contract" between each person and their society. Thus, just as we require a driving licence and car insurance to drive a car, so users of a driverless car should be required to share their data for everyone's collective good.

For this to happen, the Big Innovation Centre argues that the government needs to establish a data charter with stakeholders on what can be done with personal and business data, so that everyone will know how their data is used and not used.

This will in turn increase trust and create incentives to allow data to be shared. The US is already moving ahead with "user rights". Britain needs to introduce a "fair use" principle too."

Yves Mulkers
BI and Data Architect

Questions to Reflect On

Is it ethical to resell customer data?

Is data sharing a social benefit?

Would sharing our health data help in eradicating disease and bring longer life?

Is a data 'social contract' or data charter the way forward for everyone's collective good?

Do we need more protection or rules to safeguard our data?

NOTES

"Yesterday is history. Tomorrow is a mystery.
Today is a gift. That's why it is called the present."

Alice Morse Earle
Historian and Author

"Life isn't a matter of milestones but of moments."

Rose Kennedy
Philanthropist

"What we do today right now, will have an accumulated effect on all our tomorrows."

Alexandra Stoddard
Contemporary Philosopher, Author and Speaker

Chapter 12
Future of Data

"Be prepared for turbulence and conflict. Because you don't have change without conflict between those who want to make change and those who want to keep the old system."

Alvin Toffler
Author and Futurist

"Everything is going to be connected to cloud and data… All of this will be mediated by software."

Satya Nadella
CEO, Microsoft and Author, Hit Refresh

"Big data is going to transform how we live, how we work and how we think. It is going to help us manage our careers and lead lives of satisfaction and hope and happiness and health. So we're going to need to be careful and take big data and adjust it for our needs, our very human needs. We have to be the master of this technology, not its servant."

Kenneth Cukier
Author of Big Data: A Revolution That Will Transform How We Live, Work and Think

"There's a digital revolution taking place both in and out of government in favor of open-sourced data, innovation, and collaboration."

Kathleen Sebelius
Former United States Secretary of Health and
Human Services

"...I tell our customers is that AI (Artificial Intelligence) and specifically ML (Machine Learning) is the future of visual storytelling as companies begin to mature our HI (Human Intelligence) and KI (Knowledge Intelligence). While I see the ideas of visual storytelling as being a manual process for some time, I envision ML taking what has been done manually and making it smarter. Not only by learning from the data provided, but also by being able to utilize outside data and factors that were otherwise unavailable or the average human cannot process."

Mico Yuk
Author, Data Visualization for Dummies and
Co-Founder and CEO, BI Brainz

"I keep saying that the sexy job in the next 10 years will be statisticians, and I'm not kidding."

Hal Varian
Chief Economist, Google

"When we have all data online, it will be great for humanity. It is a prerequisite to solving many problems that humankind faces."

Robert Cailliau
Informatics Engineer and Computer Scientist who, together with Tim-Berners-Lee, developed the World Wide Web

"We should expect a 'Big Data 2.0' phase to follow 'Big Data 1.0'. Once firms have become capable of processing massive data in a flexible fashion, they should begin asking: 'What can I do that I couldn't do before, or do better than I could do before?' This is likely to be the golden era of data science."

Foster Provost and Tom Fawcett
Co-Authors, Data Science for Business

"In the next 10 years, data science and software will do more for medicine than all of the biological sciences together."

Vinod Khosla
Co-Founder of Sun Microsystems and Founder of Khosla Ventures

"Self-sovereignty of personal data will feature strongly as Web 3.0 distributed applications become more popular and widespread, completely revolutionizing the current digital advertising model."

George Zarkadakis
Digital Lead, Willis Towers Watson

"We should teach the students, as well as executives, how to conduct experiments, how to examine data, and how to use these tools to make better decisions."

Dan Ariely
Founder, The Center for Advanced Hindsight and
Co-Founder of BE works

"In 2010, foreign students received more than 50 percent of all Ph.D.s awarded in every subject in the United States. In the sciences, that figure is closer to 75 percent. Half of all Silicon Valley start-ups have one founder who is an immigrant or first-generation American. America's potential new burst of productivity, its edge in nanotechnology, biotechnology, its ability to invent the future-all rest on its immigration policies."

Fareed Zakaria
Journalist and Author, The Post-American World

"Today, every discussion about changes in technology, business, and society begins with data. In its exponentially increasing volume, velocity and variety, data is becoming a new natural resource."

Arvind Shetty
Product Manager and Director, IBM Analytics

"If you went to bed last night as an industrial company, you're going to wake up this morning as a software and analytics company."

Jeff Immelt
Former GE Chairman and CEO
(Told 100s of customers and analysts attending the 3rd
"Minds + Machines" Summit (2014))

"Big data is at the foundation of all the megatrends that are happening today, from social to mobile to the cloud to gaming."

Chris Lynch
Former Vertica CEO

"We speak of 'software eating the world', 'the Internet of Things', and we massify 'data' by declaring it 'Big'. But these concepts remain for the most part abstract. It's hard for many of us to grasp the impact of digital technology on the 'real world' of things like rocks, homes, cars and trees. We lack a metaphor that hits home."

John Battelle
Founder, Wired Magazine

"Our lives are already significantly more complex than even five years ago. We need to pay attention to far more sources in order to do our jobs, to learn, to parent, or even to be entertained. The number of factors and possibilities we have to attend to rises each year almost exponentially. Thus our seemingly permanently distracted state and our endless flitting from one thing to another is not a sign of disaster, but is a necessary adaptation to this current environment."

Kevin Kelly
Author of The Inevitable: Understanding the 12
Technological Forces That Will Shape Our Future

"Consumer data will be the biggest differentiator in the next two or three years. Whoever unlocks the reams of data and uses it strategically will win."

Angela Ahrendts
Senior Vice President of Retail, Apple

Questions to Reflect On

Has the data-driven initiative and culture been led by the CEO and senior management and/or by the Data Science team?

Assuming your organisation/business, is a data-driven culture in practice, then how is it embedding its purpose and data-driven behaviours within the workplace?

Is having open and transparent data, for all to see, great for humanity?

NOTES

"The only way to discover the limits of the possible is to go beyond them into the impossible."

Arthur C. Clarke
Science Fiction Writer, Futurist and Inventor

Conclusion

Writing this book has been an honour and a joy and I hope that as a reader, that you also learned some new facts and perspectives as I have through the many voices that spoke through this book about Data Scientists, Data Science, Machine Learning and Artificial Intelligence and of the many challenges and opportunities that exist.

The role of the Data Scientist is truly becoming one of the most important and impactful positions in the world, that is and will be changing and influencing our entire living and working existence. Data Scientists are offering us the potential to live a more prosperous, ethical, humane and respectful society – through more informed insights and innovation, for an organisation (and its staff and customers) to thrive and reach its growth potential, identify areas of inefficiency and reduction of waste and offer cleaner, faster and more transparent processes.

Their efforts are also providing improved health conditions and standards (e.g. that could solve cancer), provide relief to real-world problems (e.g. the potential to eradicate world hunger, lower traffic congestion and pollution), and alleviate customers' pain points, provide greater choice and advice for consumers and enhanced empowerment. Hence, with all the above benefits, it could also provide more openness and acceptance of other's opinions, regardless of age, gender and background and offer greater sustainability and societal impact as a result.

Conversely, recent events in the news has shaken the trust of users of social media (e.g. Cambridge Analytica, that has ties to US President's Trump 2016 campaign accessed information from 87 million Facebook users without their prior knowledge) and has again, brought to the forefront, the all pervasive issue of our rights to data privacy and how our data is to be used. Time will tell how this issue will unravel, for the over 2 billion Facebook users and for all users of social media. One of the main concerns surrounding our data is simply having trust in the organisation that possesses it and safeguarding our data for what they could do with it in the future.

Hopefully, the GDPR (General Data Protection Regulation) that will be coming into force in May 2018, which will require organisations to offer consumers greater control over how their data is stored and used will make a positive contribution towards providing greater trust, accountability and transparency.

Some of the most exciting areas in Data Science covered in the book are Machine Learning (including Deep Learning), Artificial Intelligence (AI) and Blockchain, all of which the market is starting to see real benefits, such as the initiation of blockchain proof-of-concepts, while robotics and AI will also be evaluated for their ability to improve turnaround and accuracy for clients. AI can analyse specific patterns, help with the sheer volume of data and eventually produce predictive analysis that can help all parties involved to make more informed decisions.

Ultimately, the improvement in technology, such as with AI and Machine Learning is meant to enhance people's lives and for AI to be more successful in our society, it will require as IBM's Ginni Rometty stated "a culture that can embrace and adapt to technological change."

By succeeding with this enormous challenge, organisations will be on their way to be data-driven.

The Data Scientist's role is to help guide and implement the data-driven culture and to fully utilize the advantage of managing data that will give businesses the insight they need to ensure that data is responsibly and securely handled, as well as the ability to provide customers with up-to-date information on demand. As a result, this will help to build stronger customer relationships through a better understanding of their needs, deriving new insights, generating greater savings, increasing effectiveness, ensuring the safety and security of the client's information and ultimately increasing revenue.

I hope this book has offered you the opportunity to read about Data Scientists, Data Science, the Power and Potential of Data and the many related fields of Data Science through a kaleidoscope of perspectives and how they all weave together to create a 'mosaic' of how our lives are evolving at an alarmingly rapid pace through technology.

Alongside the initial resistance and disruption that we will encounter, resilience, agility and adaptability will grow as outcomes through our experiences. Innovation will also surface and individually and collectively, we can make a positive contribution by ensuring our global society benefits from these innovative advancements and breakthroughs for the common good of all – on the road to greater health, peace and abundance.

Recommended Resources

Analytics Vidhya - https://www.analyticsvidhya.com/

Analytics Vidhya provides a community based knowledge portal for Analytics and Data Science professionals. The aim of the platform is to become a complete portal serving all knowledge and career needs of Data Science Professionals.

Data Science 101 - http://101.datascience.community/

Data Science 101 is blog, created in 2012, by Ryan Swanstrom, to share some resources for learning data science.

Data Science Association - http://www.datascienceassn.org/

The Data Science Association is a non-profit professional association of data scientists that serves its members, improving the data science profession, eliminating bias and enhancing diversity and advancing ethical data science worldwide.

Data Science Central - https://www.datasciencecentral.com/

Data Science Central is the industry's online resource for big data practitioners. From Analytics to Data Integration to Visualization, Data Science Central provides a community experience that includes a robust editorial platform, social interaction, forum-based technical support, the latest in technology, tools and trends and industry job opportunities.

Data Science Weekly - https://www.datascienceweekly.org/

Data Science Weekly is a weekly newsletter featuring curated news, articles, resources and opportunities related to Data Science.

Datatau - https://www.datatau.com

Venture Beat refers to Datatau as "Hacker News for Data Scientists," because it provides interesting articles and users share career advice for newcomers to Data Science.

FiveThirtyEight - http://fivethirtyeight.com/

FiveThirtyEight, launched by author Nate Silver, offers data analysis and visualizations of political, cultural and economic matters of the day. It shares work that is light-hearted and interactive and provides an illustration of how data can be available and applied to our daily lives.

Flowing Data - http://flowingdata.com/

Flowing Data examines how data professionals analyse and visualize data to better comprehend patterns, insights and results. The site also provides book recommendations, tutorials, a job board and a membership feature to help up and coming data scientists grow and develop their craft.

Dr. Nathan Yau offers a humorous approach on the challenges in working as a data professional, by discussing the ethical challenges in gathering data and the mistakes often made in data analysis, and how data is used to track changes and growth in society over time.

Github - https://www.github.com

GitHub is the world's leading community of developers to share and build better software (primarily used for computer code), ranging from open source projects to private team repositories. It also offers all of the distributed version control and source code management functionality of Git.

Kaggle - https://www.kaggle.com

Kaggle is a platform for data prediction competitions. One can search through a list of upcoming competitions, the website also offers a forum, where visitors can search for partners for competitions, share resources and ask for support in building a career in Data Science.

KD Nuggets - https://www.kdnuggets.com

KD Nuggets offers tutorials, articles, webinars, and information on data mining and building models. One can also subscribe to the informative bi-weekly newsletter.

No Free Hunch (Kaggle) - http://blog.kaggle.com/

No Free Hunch is the official blog of Kaggle.com.

O'Reilly Media - https://www.oreilly.com

O'Reilly Media, a media company established by Tim O'Reilly, publishes books and provides conferences on computer technology topics.

Quora - https://www.quora.com/

Quora is a question-and-answer site, where questions are asked, answered, edited and organised by its community of users.

R-Bloggers - https://www.r-bloggers.com/

R-Bloggers is a hub with content around open-source statistical software and an informative resource to follow both major trends and contributors.

There are currently over 750 blogs, concentrating on news and tutorials relating to R, which is a programming language and free software environment for statistical computing and graphics.

Simply Statistics - https://simplystatistics.org/

Simply Statistics is a Statistics blog by Rafa Irizarry, Roger Peng and Jeff Leek, all three are biostatistics professors from John Hopkins University, Harvard University and the Dana Farber Cancer Institute. The blog consists of articles about how data is being used (and misused) to resolve complex problems. The above professors also offer Data Analysis courses on Coursera and interviews with rising Data Scientists and discuss their future career options.

"Books showed me there were possibilities in life, that there were actually people like me living in a world I could not only aspire to but attain. Reading gave me hope. For me, it was the open door."

Oprah Winfrey
Media Owner, Talk Show Host,
Author and Philanthropist

Recommended Books

Alistair Croll and Benjamin Yoskovitz, *Lean Analytics: Use Data to Build a Better Startup Faster,* O'Reilly Media, 2013.

Bernard Marr, *Big Data, Using Smart Big Data Analytics and Metrics to Make Better Decisions and Improve Performance,* John Wiley & Sons, 2015.

Bernard Marr, *Big Data in Practice: How 45 Successful Companies Used Big Data Analytics to Deliver Extraordinary Results,* John Wiley & Sons, 2015.

Bernard Marr, *Data Strategy: How to Profit from a World of Big Data, Analytics and the Internet of Things*, Kogan Page, 2017.

Cathy O'Neil and Rachel Schutt, *Doing Data Science: Straight Talk from the Frontline,* O'Reilly Media, 2013.

Cathy O'Neil, *Weapons of Math Destruction: How Big Data Increases Inequality and Threatens Democracy*, Penguin Books, 2017.

Carl Shan, Henry Wang, William Chen and Max Song, *The Data Science Handbook,* The Data Science Bookshelf, 2015.

Caroline Carruthers and Peter Jackson, *The Chief Data Officer's Playbook,* Facet Publishing, 2017.

Christopher Bishop, *Pattern Recognition and Machine Learning,* Springer, 2007.

Christopher Steiner, *Automate This: How Algorithms Come to Rule Our World,* Portfolio Penguin, 2013.

Cole Nussbaumer Knaflic, *Storytelling with Data,* John Wiley & Sons, 2015.

Eric Siegel, *Predictive Analytics: The Power to Predict Who Will Click, Buy, Lie or Die,* John Wiley & Sons, 2016.

Fareed Zakaria, *The Post-American World,* W.W.Norton & Company, 2008.

Foster Provost and Tom Fawcett, *Data Science for Business,* O'Reilly Media, 2013.

Graham Hogg, *Seeing Around Corners,* LID Publishing, 2017.

John W. Foreman, *Data Smart: Using Data Science to Transform Information Into Insight,* John Wiley & Sons, 2013.

Kate Strachnyi, *Journey to Data Scientist,* CreateSpace Independent Publishing Platform, 2017.

Kevin Kelly, *The Inevitable: Understanding the 12 Technological Forces That Will Shape Our Future,* Penguin Books, 2016.

Nassim Nicholas Taleb, *Black Swan: The Impact of the Highly Improbable, Penguin Books, 2007.*

Nate Silver, *The Signal and The Noise: Why So Many Predictions Fail, But Some Don't,* Random House, 2012.

Pedro Domingos, *Master Algorithm: How the Quest for the Ultimate Learning Machine Will Remake Our World,* Penguin Books, 2015.

Ray Kurzweil, *The Singularity is Near: When Humans Transcend Biology*, Viking Press, 2005.

Roger D. Peng and Elizabeth Matsui, *The Art of Data Science*, lulu.com, 2016.

Sebastian Gutierrez, *Data Scientists at Work*, Apress, 2014.

Steve Lohr, *Dataism: Inside the Big Data Revolution*, Oneworld Publications, 2016.

Theresa M. Payton and Ted Claypoole, *Privacy in the Age of Big Data: Recognizing Threats, Defending Your Rights, and Protecting Your Family*, Rowman & Littlefield Publishers, 2014.

Thomas H. Davenport and Jinho Kim, *Keeping Up with the Quants: Your Guide to Understanding and Using Analytics*, Harvard Business Review, 2013.

Thomas H. Davenport, *Big Data at Work: Dispelling the Myths, Uncovering the Opportunities*, Harvard Business Review, 2014.

Tomasz Tunguz and Frank Bien, *Winning with Data: Transform Your Culture, Empower Your People, and Shape the Future*, John Wiley & Sons, 2016.

Viktor Mayer-Schönberger and Kenneth Cukier, *Big Data: A Revolution That Will Transform How We Live, Work and Think*, John Murray, 2013.

Vincent Granville, *Developing Analytic Talent*, John Wiley & Sons, 2014.

Zacharias Voulgaris, *Data Scientist*, Technics Publications, 2014.

"Now more than ever we need to talk to each other, and understand how we see the world, and cinema is the best medium for doing this."

Martin Scorsese
Film Director, Producer and Screenwriter

'Data Science' Films

Metropolis, 1927

2001: A Space Odyssey, 1968

Colussus: The Forbin Project, 1970

Star Wars, 1977

Blade Runner, 1982

Star Trek: Generations, 1994

Bicentennial Man, 1999

The Matrix, 1999

A.I. Artificial Intelligence, 2001

A Beautiful Mind, 2002

Minority Report, 2002

21, 2008

Moneyball, 2011

Her, 2013

The Imitation Game, 2014

Chappie, 2015

Ex Machina, 2015

The Big Short, 2016

"Each of us is a unique strand in the intricate web of life and here to make a contribution."

Deepak Chopra
Author and Speaker

Contributors

Aaron Koblin

Adam Savage

Albert Einstein

Aldous Huxley

Alex Morritt

Alex Peiniger

Alexander Linden

Alexandra Stoddard

Alice Morse Earle

Alistair Croll

Alvin Toffler

Amy Heineike

Anna Smith

Andre Karpistsenko

Andreas Weigend

Andrew Ng

Angela Ahrendts

Aristotle

Arthur C. Clarke

Arthur C. Nielsen

Arthur Conan Doyle

Arun Singhal

Arvind Shetty

Atul Butte

Ayn Rand

Beau Walker

Benjamin Yoskovitz

Bernard Marr

Bill Gates

Bill Maris

Bill Schmarzo

Billy Beane

Bob Hayes

Brad Gammons

Brad Stone

Bradley Voytek

Caitlin Smallwood

Carla Gentry

Carly Fiorina

Cathy O'Neil

Charles Babbage

Chip Heath

Chris Arnold

Chris Bell

Chris Lynch

Chris Moody

Chris Pehura

Chris Wiggins

Clare Corthell

Claudia Perlich

Clayton M. Christensen

Clifford Stoll

Cole Nussbaumer Knaflic

Craig Mundie

Curt Davis

Damian Mingle

Dan Ariely

Dan Heath

Daniel Keys Moran

Daniel Tunkelang

David McCandless

Deepak Chopra

Dennis R. Mortensen

Dez Blanchfield

Diane Wu

DJ Patil

Douglas Merrill

Douglas Rushkoff

Drew Conway

Eckhart Tolle

Edwin Chen

Eithon Cadag

Eleanor Roosevelt

Elon Musk

Eric Schmidt

Eric Siegel

Erin LeDell

Erin Shellman

Fareed Zakaria

Fred Hoyle

Foster Provost

Geoffrey Hinton

Geoffrey Moore

George Packer

George Roumeliotis

George Zarkadakis

Ginni Rometty

Graham Hogg

Gray Scott

Gregory Piatetsky-Shapiro

Hadley Wickham

Hal Varian

Hilary Mason

Isaac Newton

Jack Welch

Jake Porway

James Barrat

James Kobielus

James O'Shaughnessy

James Scott

Jamie Dimon

Jatin Solanki

Jean-Paul Isson

Jeff Bezos

Jeff Immelt

Jeff Weiner

Jennifer Pahlka

Jennifer Shin

Jim Rohn

John Battelle

John Dryden

John Foreman

John W. Foreman

Jonathan Lenaghan

Jonathan Rosenberg

Jose Ferreira

Josh Wills

Jürgen Schmidhuber

Karolis Urbonas

Kate Strachnyi

Kathleen Sebelius

Kenneth Cukier

Kevin Kelly

Kevin Novak

Kirk Borne

Klaus Schwab

Kurt Bollacker

Larry Page

Lutz Finger

Mahatma Gandhi

Marc Benioff

Margaret Thatcher

Margot Gerritsen

Marian Wright Edelman

Mark Cuban

Mark Zuckerberg

Marshall McLuhan

Martin Luther King, Jr

Martin Scorsese

Martyn Jones

Mary Leakey

Matei Zahaira

Matt Corey

Matthew Oczkowski

Max Kuhn

Max Levchin

Maya Angelou

McKinsey Report – Big Data: The next frontier for innovation, competition, and productivity

Meta S. Brown

Michael Hochster

Michael O'Connell

Michelangelo D'Agostino

Mico Yuk

Mike Dewar

Mike Krieger

Mike Loukides

Mikko Hypponen

Monica Rogati

Narendra Modi

Nate Silver

Neil deGrasse Tyson

Neil Raden

Nick Bilton

Nick Bostrom

Oprah Winfrey

Oren Etzioni

Patrick P. Gelsinger

Pete Skomoroch

Peter Diamandis

Peter Sondergaard

Peter Thiel

Piyush Kumar Chowhan

Pramod Singh

Rachel Schutt

Ratnakar Pandey

Ray Kurzweil

Riley Newman

Robert Cailliau

Robert J. Shiller

Roger Ehrenberg

Ronald Fisher

Rose Kennedy

Ruth Porat

Sarah Ban Breathnach

Satya Nadella

Scott Nicholson

Sean Gourley

Sean Rad

Sebastian Gutierrez

Sebastian Thrun

Sendhil Mullainathan

Shanji Xiong

Shelly D. Farnham

Shiva Rajaraman

Sophocles

Stephan Kolassa

Stephen Few

Stephen Hawking

Steve Jurvetson

References

www.artificialintelligencehow.com

https://todayinsci.com/QuotationsCategories/D_Cat/Data-Quotations.htm

https://www.springboard.com/blog/41-shareable-data-quotes/

http://uk.businessinsider.com/jeff-bezos-shareholder-letter-on-ai-and-machine-learning-2017-4

https://www.goodreads.com/quotes/tag/machine-learning

www.brainyquote.com/search_results?q=machine+learning

https://www.brainyquote.com/authors/steve_jurvetson

https://analyticsindiamag.com/a-compilation-of-20-insightful-quotes-from-indian-analytics-leaders/

https://www.statistics.com/landing-page/data-science/data-science-quotes/

https://www.slideshare.net/BernardMarr/big-data-best-quotes/

https://www.datasciencecentral.com/profiles/blogs/20-quotes-from-a-data-science-pioneer

http://blog.millionlights.org/2017/06/20/quotes-on-data-science-from-leaders/

http://bigdata-madesimple.com/10-data-science-big-data-experts-follow-twitter/

https://www.tibco.com/blog/2013/06/28/19781/

https://www.goodreads.com/quotes/tag/data-science

http://www.ibtimes.co.uk/political-revolution-how-big-data-won-us-presidency-donald-trump-1602269

http://fortune.com/2014/10/10/ge-data-robotics-sensors/

https://www.sisense.com/blog/12-quotes-data-science-thought-leaders/

http://bigdata-madesimple.com/30-tweetable-quotes-data-science/

https://www.springboard.com/blog/41-shareable-data-quotes/

https://www.kdnuggets.com/2017/05/42-essential-quotes-data-science-thought-leaders.html/

https://goo.gl/yeEQhQ

www.foxydatascience.com

https://whatsthebigdata.com/2012/07/20/big-data-quotes-of-the-week-july-20-2012/

https://medium.com/future-of-work/data-is-the-fuel-for-ai-so-lets-ensure-we-get-the-ethics-right-b15337e18081

http://fortune.com/2016/05/23/jamie-dimon-data-misuse/

https://www.ndtv.com/india-news/prime-minister-narendra-modis-top-quotes-at-davos-world-economic-forum-1803657

https://bowen0701.github.io/2015/07/12/airbnb-data-science/

https://databricks.com/blog/2018/01/17/matei-zaharias-5-predictions-about-ai-in-2018.html

https://www.forbes.com/sites/quora/2017/06/15/what-are-the-top-five-skills-data-scientists-need/amp/

http://www.brightidea.com/blog/10-articles-that-redefined-innovation-in-2014/

https://www.promptcloud.com/jurgen-schmidhuber-artificial-intelligence-future

https://www.brainyquote.com/quotes/steve_jobs_416859

https://www.jellyfish.co.uk/news-and-views/digital-journeys-2017-emily-booth-ibm

https://engineering.stanford.edu/magazine/article/how-data-analytics-going-transform-all-industries

https://www.kdnuggets.com/2015/04/data-scientists-thoughts-that-inspire.html

https://datascience.berkeley.edu/what-is-big-data/

http://fortune.com/2017/10/24/walmart-ai-startup-primer/

http://www.jeannicholashould.com/what-is-a-data-scientist.html

https://www.thriveglobal.com/stories/25002-12-rich-powerful-people-share-their-surprising-definitions-of-success

https://www.forbes.com/sites/metabrown/2018/01/30/he-turned-data-storytelling-success-into-data-storytelling-failure-heres-what-went-wrong/#36c2b04848a5

https://blog.udacity.com/2014/12/24-data-science-resources-keep-finger-pulse.html

https://en.wikipedia.org/wiki/Thomas_Edison

https://leadmastersblog.com/2018/01/02/5-ways-powerful-impressive-leaders-describe-success/

https://www.springboard.com/blog/machine-learning-interview-questions/

https://www.inc.com/john-brandon/heres-why-you-will-be-hiring-a-data-scientist-in-2016.html

https://mathbabe.org/2011/09/25/why-and-how-to-hire-a-data-scientist-for-your-business/

https://growthhackers.com/amas/mico-yuk-co-founder-ceo-bi-brainz-author-keynote-speaker

https://www.jstatsoft.org/article/view/v059i10/v59i10.pdf

http://appliedpredictivemodeling.com/blog/2013/5/20/one-statisticians-view-of-big-data

https://mlconf.com/interview-with-erin-ledell-machine-learning-scientist-h2o-ai/

https://www.favouriteblog.com/best-quotes-artificial-intelligence/

www.indiewire.com

www.ranker.com/list

www.theguardian.com/culture

www.analyticsvidhya.com/blog

About the Author

MATT COREY is a Recruitment and Human Resources professional with 15 years of successful achievements within various industries in the private, public and third sectors.

Matt graduated with a B.A., M.Sc. in Psychology and a Postgraduate degree in Human Resources and became a Member (MCIPD) of the Chartered Institute of Personnel and Development (CIPD). He is also a qualified Change Management Practitioner and Coach.

As the leader of Change Force, an exclusive niche Data Scientist Recruitment Practice, he is committed and passionate to helping organisations achieve sustainability and reach their growth potential through Data Scientists and their respective contributions to making a positive impact within the marketplace and society.

He is available for talks and conferences on the subjects of Data Science, Corporate Sustainability and Impact, Talent Management and Employee Integration of Data Scientists.

Matt lives in London, United Kingdom and you can visit the company website at www.changeforceinc.com.